D1328393

Dynamic Taekwondo Kyŏrugi

Dynamic Taekwondo
Kyŏrugi

Kyong Myong Lee

HOLLYM
Elizabeth, NJ · SEOUL

Maysville Community College
Library

GU
1114.9
.L4370
1996

Copyright © 1996
by Kyong Myong Lee

All rights reserved.

First published in 1996
by Hollym International Corp.
18 Donald Place, Elizabeth, NJ 07208, U.S.A.
Tel: (908)353-1655   Fax: (908)353-0255

Published simultaneously in Korea
by Hollym Corporation; Publishers
14-5, Kwanchol-dong, Chongno-gu, Seoul 110-111, Korea
Tel: (02)734-5087   Fax: (02)730-8192

ISBN: 1-56591-069-9
Library of Congress Catalog Card Number:96-78906

Printed in Korea

THE WORLD TAEWKONDO FEDERATION

635 YUKSAM-DONG, KANGNAM-KU, SEOUL, KOREA 135-080 TEL:(82-2) 566-2505, 557-5446 FAX:(82-2) 553-4728

September 1996

I congratulate Grand Master Kyong Myong Lee on the release of Dynamic Taekwondo Kyŏrugi. *This is one of the books he has written on Taekwondo and a sport and a martial art.*

Taekwondo has become a global sport. It is an official program of 2000 Sydney Olympic Games as well as a major multi-sport and continental games. Besides these games, Taekwondo has celebrated the events of its own at the world level such as World Championships, World Junior Championships, World University Championships and World Military Championships. Also, continental and sub-continental Taekwondo championships have been held with international and goodwill tournament organized by different countries.

Kyŏrugi (sparring) is one of the three elements of Taekwondo together with P'umsae (basic stances or movements) and Kyŏkp'a (breaking). The aspect of Taekwondo as a game sport has been growingly emphasized in the course of extension and propagation of Taekwondo to the whole world through these competitions. Now we need to devise a systematic training method

THE WORLD TAEWKONDO FEDERATION

635 YUKSAM-DONG, KANGNAM-KU, SEOUL, KOREA 135-080 TEL:(82-2) 566-2505, 557-5446 FAX:(82-2) 553-4728

for competitions which includes innate Oriental ideas of Taekwondo as a martial art. In the way we could develop Taekwondo in both appearance and substance.

Taekwondo is not a simple combat sport. Its performance requires techniques and a certain state of mind. Physical and mental discipline in Taekwondo training improves the practitioner himself/herself and the society which he/she belongs to. I commend Grand Master Kyong Myong Lee for his effort toward the development of Taekwondo in the theoretical aspect and hope this would be a great use to Taekwondo athletes and coaches.

Dr. Un Yong Kim
President, WTF

Official Sport in 2000 Sydney Olympic Games

Grand Master Kyong Myong Lee

Master Lee, a Kukkiwon-authorized 9th-tan Black-belter, has a licence of Qualification for Coaching issued by Austrian authority. He has served as a Deputy Secretary General of World Taekwondo Federation since 1991 and is a member of the Contemporary Essay Literature Association.

● Major Career

· Vice President, Austria Taekwondo Association
· Chairman, Technical Committee of ATA
· Manager, Coach and Trainer, Austrian Taekwondo Teams
· Permanent Member, Test Committee for Polish Taekwondo Association
· Manager, Polish National Taekwondo Team
· Chairman, Technical Committee of European Taekwondo Union
· Member, WTF Technical Committee
· Coach, Austrian National Taekwondo Team for 1988 Seoul Olympiad
  Lecturer, National Academy for Coaches (Austria)

● Educational Background

· Yonsei University (B.A. Philosophical Science)
· Graduate Course of Yonsei University (Press and Public Relations)
· Honorary Doctorate, Lipetsk State Pedagogical Institute Russia Present

● Written Accomplishment

· Essays: Grounds of Cognition and Yearning
          Roving through the World
          The Way of a Philosophical Martial-art Man

· Texts: Richtig Taekwondo (Munich, 1987)
         Taekwondo (Warsaw, 1989)
         Taekwondo Kyorugi (Hartford, 1994)
         Dynamic Taekwondo (Seoul, New Jersey, 1995)
         Taekwondo (New York, 1996)
         Taekwondo Kyorugi (Seoul, 1996)

The three essential elements to constitute Taekwondo are P'umsae, Kyŏkp'a and Kyŏrugi. Of them, kyŏrugi has developed individually its own character to become a global sport and an official sport of the Sydney 2000 Olympic Games.

Kyŏrugi, having advanced its style to competition sport, is being competed by elite players in more and more competitions nationally and internationally.

Major factors to form competition ability are technique, physical strength and strategy. However, it tends to place its precedence in the order of physical strength, technique and strategy.

Competitors' promotion in competition power can be acquired through harmonization both of theoretical and practical training: a scientific study progress of sport. Compared with Taekwondo's stage in the sport world it is, relatively, true fact that Taekwondo study materials such as textbook, guidebook for leaders, coached or trainers, competitors are not much sufficient in number.

Based on long career of teaching as a master and diverse experiences, I carried in this book all kinds of theoretical and practical knowledges on kyŏrugi. Considering the current situation in the lack of literature for Taekwondo teaching and learning, I feel proud and self-conceit about this edition to which I added more beneficial information as much as possible in reference to the former one I published under the joint authorship a few years ago.

It is my deep wish this book be read through by all Taekwondoists and be recognized as an excellent guidebook to everyone. Also, I hope it will be a part of contribution to the sound development of Taekwondo competition culture.

My special acknowledgement goes to Master Hyok Chang, champion tow times of the World Taekwondo Championships and Master N. Kwon Hyung, teaching students in the United State, for their kind cooperation with this publication. Also my deepest respects go to President Dr. Un Yong Kim and Secretary General Kum Hong Lee of the World Taekwondo Federation who contributed greatly themselves to the globalization of Taekwondo.

With best wishes for incessant prosperity in the future development of Olympic sport Taekwondo,

In Fall, 1996

Kyong Myong Lee

Table of Contents

Table of Contents

Chapter 1 ONE

Understanding of
Taekwondo Competition

Philosophical Concepts and Conceptual Framework of Taekwondo

Taekwondo is more than a fighting skill. It is a method and a way for each one of us to pursue our lives.

.Training in Taekwondo has more value than just the athletic activity itself. From a different perspective, the training and practicing can both improve and increase the capacities of the human mind and body. Taekwondo training can most definitely provide more than mind/body cultivation: it is a meaningful concept of philosophical expression. This specific feature of Taekwondo (training and practice) is seen as one unit.

The 'unity of mind and body' concept relates to human character. So then the purpose of Taekwondo training is the striving for the ideal level of completion and the attainment taught and practiced in the tojang.

Therefore, Taekwondo is an exercise of the entire body and mind, as well as mental training that will help each of us improve and make progress with our human character. The real purpose of Taekwondo training is to improve our characteristics. Taekwondo is a very practical way to achieve this goal.

"Taekwon" in Taekwondo means 'skillful form,' which is training on the physical aspect of the meaning. In contrast, "do" in Taekwondo means 'metaphysical.' Therefore, Taekwondo contains both theoretical as well as practical sides. "Do" remains within each one of us. Consistent training and practice will help us improve ourselves. That helps us to make more realizations than ever before. Put a different way, Taekwondo training and practice is the way or method to help us improve ourselves through consistent training and practice, and in the process we learn to deal with ourselves more effectively by overcoming the difficulties and thus become better person.

Meditation is an essential method in mental training of Taekwondo. In meditation, we should have an introspective focus and analyze each level of our mind. The meditation is the practical way to deal with and improve our mental state as well as our characters. Through Taekwondo training, we discipline our body and mind, obtain peace of mind, and finally reach the state in which mind and body become one. Through meditation, we recognize the principles of the universe and nature and learn how to adapt ourselves to the universal order. Practicing "do" — the way — is aimed at achieving such a state and the ultimate goal of the martial artist is to achieve realization of this humane life.

Taekwondo has three words combined.

"Tae (태)" is a system of techniques with the feet.

"Kwon (권)" is a system of techniques with the hands.

"Do (도)" is a behavioral intuition obtained through mental and physical experiences (training, kyŏrugi, competition, etc.) of the systems of fist and foot techniques.

This means the internal perfection of a self by self-disciplined attitude through Taekwondo practice. Kyŏrugi (Taekwondo Sparring) is an important part of training that will help us deal with real situations. Today, sparring in Taekwondo has become an individual competitive sport.

Kyŏrugi can be considered a one-to-one fighting sport.

There are three parts in Taekwondo.

1. P'umsae — Form/Pattern
2. Kyŏkp'a — Breaking
3. Kyŏrugi — Sparring/Fighting

As I mentioned earlier, sparring in Taekwondo has become sports oriented, and became official in 1988 at the Seoul Olympics and in 1992 at the Barcelona Olympics. Taekwondo was adopted as an official program of 2000 Sydney Olympic Games.

But the ultimate winner in Taekwondo is the one who can win over himself or herself.

Kyŏrugi, therefore, helps us establish a rule in dealing with ourselves.

The answer to "What is Taekwondo?", then, is: Taekwondo is a practical activity and a philosophical activity to accomplish a martial art.

2

Courtesy

"Ye (예)" is an abbreviation for 'Yeŭi (예의).' 'Ye' is the most important and fundamental standard for every human being. In other words, courtesy is considered a model of a basic behavior of civilization.

In Taekwondo, doing ye (bowing to each other in the tojang is an example of ye), is important for us to maintain good body posture and, more importantly, we should show our respect to our opponent. Ye is deeply rooted in Confucianism and is put much emphasis in martial arts. Martial art training start and ends with this "ye" in all martial arts, including Taekwondo.

Taekwondo has strict courtesy. First, senior belters are courteous to lower belters. Also, then, fellow members in every class as well. Taekwondo practitioners should start with this courtesy in an ethical and moral way. In Taekwondo, most courtesy is carried and shown while you are standing.

• Whether dealing with a higher or lower belt, always carry yourself in an appreciative manner.

• You should have an upright manner when you carry ye.

• Bow from the waist at a 15-20 degree angle.

■ Yeŭibŏpto (예의법도) — Rules of Courtesy

• When entering the tojang, bow before walking on the floor. When leaving, bow before walking off the floor.

• The tojang is the place where the practitioner learns his/her skills and practices the training and discipline of mind and body and improving character. So the tojang is where all the educational training is carried on; therefore, all Taekwondo practitioners should maintain an appreciative attitude when they enter and leave the tojang. When you bow to a teacher or instructor, or to your junior belter or student, it is important to do so with respect and trust.

• This courtesy (respect and trust) will help us to develop our mental cultivation. However, during practice, treat your partner as educational partner who will help you improve. Therefore, we maintain this courtesy.

3

Structure of Kyŏrugi and Competition

Kyŏrugi is usually done on a one-to-one basis using all the skills you have learned in the tojang. Timing and distance are fundamentally important. Kyŏrugi is done between two practitioner. Their 'ki' and skills are exchanged in time and distance through their kicks and punches interchanged. Competition means a special fundamental characteristic of sports which contains the special character of games. Therefore, sports games contain or retain a component of competition. Sports originally contained a game-like play. Play games and competition combine all three to present a sport.

Taekwondo competition means Kyŏrugi, which is "sportized" sparring.

■ Main factors for sportization of Taekwondo

• No fist attacks to the face

• No attacks below belt level (waist or lower)

• No throwing or grabbing techniques

• Wear protective equipment

• Evaluation (scoring) of techniques mainly by the hitting power

Kyŏrugi contains a great deal of risk of injury. Kyŏrugi training must be done in the tojang under the authorized supervision of a qualified person and no contact sparring is allowed. No contact sparring means you shorten or pull the punch or kick just before hitting the opponent.

■ Adjusted Kyŏrugi

Adjusted Kyŏrugi is to train offensive and defensive techniques of Taekwondo based on a certain form with a partner. It is the basic part of exercise Kyŏrugi and is an early stage of training. This Kyŏrugi is aimed at improving general abilities, including timing, concentration, distance control, change of techniques, and body movements.

• One set Kyŏrugi
• Three sets Kyŏrugi

■ Exercise Kyŏrugi (Learning Kyŏrugi)

Exercise Kyŏrugi is to improve the factors of competition (speed, agility, feint, footwork, etc.) in the situation of a real competition by performing allowed techniques to the real opponent. Practice of Kyŏrugi fosters fighting spirit, courage and vigor and improves hoshinsul (self defense art).

■ Match Kyŏrugi (Competition Kyŏrugi)

This Kyŏrugi is a sport activity in which athletes wear protective equipment under the competition rules and evaluation of techniques by scoring system decides the result of the game. In this Kyŏrugi physical strength, technical superiority, tactics, mental strength, etc., are the essential factors of the games result.

Today protective equipment has been developed for the safety of competitors as Taekwondo has been sportized. In particular, the trunk protector provides a target as well as safety. Competition Taekwondo is a whole-body contact sport in which its typical structure of attack-defense-counterattack was transformed to the structure of attack-counterattack, that is kicks-counterkicks.

A counterkick is structurally decided in a reaction to a kick. The most important body movement to enable this kick-counterkick structure is footwork. Development of this footwork is the essence which enables the transformation to tempo-spatial aesthetics. It is considered a dynamism of Taekwondo.

In the footwork in which two athletes fight each other, Taekwondo Kyŏrugi consists of changes in tempo-spatial structures like front kicks, back kicks, turning forward, turning backward, moving forward or backward, and turning aside, etc., in closed and open situations (variable forms).

Taekwondo Kyŏrugi requires surprising development of kicking techniques and is accompanied by speed and hitting power of kicks and highly tactical thinking.

4

Mental Attitude in Competition

This means the sportsmanship raised through Taekwondo competitions. Sportsmanship in Taekwondo competition requires a fair play which contains strict observance of the competition rules, truth and sincerity. This fair play is the base of competition rules of Taekwondo and has internal characters like morality and ethics.

Important mental attitudes required:

- Abide by the rules.
- Do the best.
- Be impartial.
- Respect the opponent.

Here, attitude in competition contains the following contents:

■ Attitude to the opponent

Taekwondo competition area is the real tojang where you can find the true self and meaningful partner in a place of severe sparring through competition. The opponent of a competitor is the partner who fulfills his/her will. It is important to respect the opponent, discern his/her ability and tactics, and match skills against him/her in a fair play spirit.

■ Attitude to the game's result

There is a result in competitions. In Taekwondo competition, you learn various offensive and defensive techniques in competition sparring which seeks for technical ideals of Taekwondo. You should do your best to fight against your opponent in a reaction to constantly changing movements of the opponent. Irrespective of the result of the games, the competitor should congratulate on the winner's success and express pity to loser's failure, from which competitors can show the beautiful dignity.

■ Attitude to the referee

Behave yourself to the referee with trust and tolerance.

Taekwondo competition adopted the competition method in a maximum consideration of safety and technical values based on traditionally sought ideas of technologies and essential technologies of Taekwondo.

The referee should manage the competition in a way that competitors seeks for ideal harmony and development of physical strength, techniques, tactics and coordination and fairly decide on the winner. The competitor should have sense of righteousness, responsibility, obedient and right attitude to the referee's authority.

■ Attitude to the competition rules

Competitors should understand the contents of competition rules well. The competition area is a place where techniques are performed with their best and an educational value of the perfection of humanity is realized. They have to keep this deep in mind during the competition. Full understanding and abiding by the general rules is the base of the fair play.

5

Development of Competition

Taekwondo is a Korean traditional martial art. T'aekkyŏn had been practiced as a folk game from the old Korea. Taekwondo of the modern times has been developed from this T'aekkyŏn. Practice of this traditional Korean martial art was prohibited during the colonialization by the Japanese imperialism for 36 years.

During the Japanese colonialism, Japan tried to connect Taekwondo with Japanese Karate by changing the name of Taekwondo to Kongsudo and Tangsudo in an aim to demolish Taekwondo. With the liberalization in 1945, however, many martial artists began to make much effort to enhance and develop the organized and unified Korean traditional martial art of Taekwondo as a sport.

The name "Taekwondo" was adopted at the 11-member Name Regulation Committee on April 11, 1955, but was used by a few sects only at that time. Korean T'aesudo (later renamed as Taekwondo in 1965) Association was established in 1961 and the 43rd National Athletic Meet held in 1963 adopted it as an official sport. Taekwondo began to be widely propagated since then, which made this time as an official beginning in the history of Taekwondo competition.

As Taekwondo becomes more sports-oriented, the training method in every tojang becomes more on a competitive basis which is the transformation of the traditional sparring based on hoshinsul meaning self-defense.

In 1959, a group of the army Taekwondo demonstration team was dispatched to Vietnam and Taiwan to perform. In the 1960's many Taekwondo masters moved to many different countries and taught Taekwondo, which became the roots of internationalized Taekwondo.

In 1973, the first World Taekwondo Championships was conducted in Seoul, Korea and 19 national teams competed. It was then that the World Taekwondo Federation (WTF) was organized.

The World Taekwondo Championships is conducted every two years and the Women's World Taekwondo Championships became official in 1987 in Barcelona. This was the 8th World Taekwondo Championships and the 1st Women's World Taekwondo Championships.

The World Taekwondo Federation is located in Seoul where the Kukkiwon and Taekwondo Academy are also located.

A total of 143 national members are affiliated to the WTF. The WTF has been recognized and accepted as the sole organization of its martial art from the General Association of International Sports Federations (GAISF).

6

Rules of Competition

Taekwondo, as has been stated numerous times, started in Korea and now it has become a popular sport event and a regular program of the Olympic Games in Sydney, Australia in the year 2000.

The WTF has been accepted and recognized by the International Olympic Committee (IOC). The WTF was organized in 1973 and as of 1996 seven revisions have been made in its rules of competition.

Understanding the rules correctly is necessary for the competitors, coaches, and trainers.

Particularly, the coaches need to obtain the updated information on the competition rules so that he/she can provide this information to the competitors.

Since Taekwondo has become an Olympic sport, the Korean language and terminology was recognized and accepted as the fourth official Olympic language. Terms of Taekwondo competition, of course, are Korean.

Maysville Community College
Library

■ Basic Terms:

Ch'aryŏt: attention
Kyŏngrye: bow
Chunbi: ready
Shijak: begin
Kŭman: stop
Kalyŏ: break
Chwa-u-hyang-u: face each other
Kyesok: continue
Kyŏnggo: warning
Kamchŏm: deduction point
Kyeshi: count time

■ Competition Area

The competition area is a 12m × 12m flat, square without any obstacles. The area is covered with an elastic mat. On the 12m × 12m mat, in the center there is an 8m × 8m square which is the contest area. Outside of the 8m × 8m is called the alert area. The alert area is marked in different colors.

■ Position of the Judges

Referee: placed in the center of the competitive area, facing towards the jury, 1.5meters away

Judges: located 50 centimeters behind where two lines meet, outside the corner

Head of Court: 1m behind on the left side, 3m apart

Contestants: 1m away to the left and the right, right side is called Ch'ŏng (blue) and the left side Hong (red)

Coach: Ch'ŏng or Hong will be located 1m outside the boundary of each contestant's side.

■ Costume

Uniform: contestants must wear tobok that are certified, and also certified protective equipment

Protective Equipment: trunk protector, head gear, forearm and shin guards, men's and women's groin guard, must be worn inside the tobok

■ Weight Divisions

There are eight weight categories each for men and women.

Weight categories	male	female
Fin	- 50kg	- 43kg
Fly	- 54kg	- 47kg
Bantam	- 58kg	- 51kg
Feather	- 64kg	- 55kg
Light	- 70kg	- 60kg
Welter	- 76kg	- 65kg
Middle	- 83kg	- 70kg
Heavy	+83kg	+ 70kg

In Olympic Games, however, there will be only four weight categories for both men and women.

Male	- 58kg	- 68kg	- 80kg	+ 80kg
Female	- 49kg	- 57kg	- 67kg	+ 67kg

■ Duration of contest

Three rounds with three minutes each. One minute break between each round.

■ Weigh-in

The contestant must weigh in one hour before the competition. If the contestant is below or above the required weight, the contestant can reweigh one more within the time.

■ Classification & Methods of Competition

• Individual competition: normally between contestants in the same weight class. When necessary, adjoining weight classes may be combined to create a single weight class.

• Team: 5 - contestants with no weight limit
         8 - contestants by weight classification
         4 - contestants by weight classification

• Methods of competition: - Single elimination tournament system
                          - Round robin system.

■ Evaluation

When you score, you get one point. You add up all three together to determine the winner. Obtaining points is based on the accuracy and power that are delivered to the opponent. There are prohibited areas on the body. If a contestant were to attack that area, negative points are given or the contestant will be disqualified within three rounds.

- Kyŏnggo (Warning) penalties

1) Grabbing the opponent
2) Pushing the opponent with the shoulder, body, hand or arms
3) Holding the opponent with hands or arms
4) Intentionally crossing the alert line
5) Evading by turning the back to the opponent
6) Intentionally falling down
7) Pretending injury
8) Attacking with the knee
9) Intentionally attacking the groin
10) Intentionally stomping or kicking any part of the leg or foot
11) Hitting the opponent's face with hands or fist
12) Gesturing to indicate scoring or deduction by raising hand, etc.
13) Uttering undesirable remarks or any misconduct on the part of the contestant or the coach

- Kamchŏm penalties

1) Attacking the fallen opponent
2) Intentionally attacking after the Referee's declaration of Kallyŏ
3) Attacking the back and the back of the head intentionally
4) Attacking the opponent's face severely with hands or fist
5) Butting
6) Crossing the boundary line
7) Throwing the opponent
8) Violent or extreme remarks or behavior on the part of the contestant or the coach

Chapter 2 TWO

Ability in Competition

1

Structure

Competing ability is the ability performed in competitions. Taekwondo competition is one-on-one combat sport. The result of the competition by points scored by accurate and powerful attacks to the permitted areas of the opponent.

Behaviors of the contestant in the Taekwondo competitions are in principle;
• being conducted by the subjective will (attacks) and at the same time.
• being done by the effect from the opponent (counterattacks).

Therefore, characteristics of the competition is that competition tasks are set up by the situations made between the two competing contestants — Ch'ŏng (Blue) and Hong (Red) contestants — and responses to the changes of the situation based on speedy tactical thinking are required. The prerequisite of the solution of tasks in competitions is the management of the competition which is appropriate effective in a situation.

Researches of competing ability should be made in a way to establish and develop methods of training appropriate to characteristics of specified Taekwondo techniques. Taekwondo techniques should be performed in actual competitions together with right tactics.

The ultimate purpose of the competitor in the competition is the accomplishment of the competition. This can be obtained by improving the competing ability and effective use of the ability.

■ Prerequisites for improving the competing ability:

- Confirmation and analysis of the problems
- Establishment of the project
- Implementation

■ Factors of the competing ability:

- Techniques
- Physical strength
- Tactics
- Coordination
- Mental fitness

■ Success in sports can be achieved by

- Improvement of techniques and tactics through continuous and repeated training
- Maintenance of appropriate arousal level which enables the successful management of the game under the strain.

2

`Techniques

Techniques are the methods to solve the competition tasks. Mental characters like awareness and analysis of the situation and tactical factors to think and solve the competition tasks are decisive in techniques. These are very important in improving ability in Taekwondo competition.

Recognition, mastering and perfection of techniques are the important content of training of Taekwondo techniques. Strong physical strength is needed for mastering excellent techniques. In Taekwondo competition, in particular, it is effective to learn techniques by strengthening speed, flexibility, agility, and coordination.

■ Basic techniques of Taekwondo competition are largely divided as follows:

• Ch'agi (Kicks: foot techniques): Kicking the target on the opponent with the feet. Attacks are made with the stretching or bending power of the knee joint.

• Chitki (Footwork): Moving one foot or two feet or changing the balance to effectively making offensive or defensive movements in Taekwondo Kyŏrugi. This is the important basic technique of Taekwondo Kyŏrugi.

• Tchirŭgi (Punch: hand techniques): Attacking the scoring area of the opponent's trunk with the fist.

• Makki (Blocks): Blocking mainly with the wrist. This is made rather by covering the scoring area from the opponent's attacks than by blocking in actual competitions.

• Sogimsu (Feint): There is a limitation in techniques in Taekwondo competition. Techniques of Taekwondo competition are very different from those of Taekwondo as a martial art. Competition techniques are always performed in recognition of the presence of the opponent, that is, in an aim to score points by hitting the target (scoring areas).

■ Targets of attacks

• Face: Front part of the face on the basis of a coronal line at both ears. Foot techniques only allowed.

• Trunk: Front part of the trunk, including both sides. Foot and hand techniques allowed.

(1) Kyŏrumsae (Standard Fighting Stance)

Kyŏrumsae is an abbreviation of Kyŏrugi stance of Taekwondo. It indicates the position the fighter assumes during the competition. Competitors should try to master the right stances in basic training so that the center of gravity may be easily changed.

Kyŏrumsae becomes a little bit different according to the physical and mental characters of the competitor.

■ Tips (Requirements)

• Flexibility: Maintaining flexibility is needed to allow movements to all body axis and all directions.
• Natural body posture
• Agility
• Base: Wide base enough to maintain balance in all movements and at rest
• Concealment: Hide the intention and initiation of offensive movements
• Center of gravity: Raise the effect of attacks and defenses by changing the center of gravity

■ Methods

• Slightly clench the fist
• Maintain two arms bent in front of the trunk
• Keep forearms and backs of the hands outward
• Develop special movements and appropriate Kyŏrumsae of one's own through long experience of competitions

■ Types of Kyŏrumsae

Basic stances of Taekwondo are generally divided by the stances of competitors during the competition. They are as follows:

① Kyŏrumsae

This is the standard Kyŏrumsae and is the prototype of all types of Kyŏrumsae. Based on the position of the rear foot, this Kyŏrumsae is divided as either right-handed Kyŏrumsae or left-handed Kyŏrumsae.

• Posture of the body: Turn approximately 45 degrees to the side
• Distance between two feet: Approximately one and a half times the regular stride
• Techniques preferred: All techniques are easily performed

② Yŏp-Kyŏrumsae (Side Fighting Stance)

This is a variation of the standard Kyŏrumsae.

• Posture of the body: To the side
• Distance between two feet: Approximately one and a half or two times the regular stride
• Techniques preferred: Side kicks and back kicks

③ Natch'umsae (Low Fighting Stance)

This is an abbreviation of lowered Kyŏrumsae and is a variation of the standard Kyŏrumsae.

• Posture of the body: Slightly to the side. Especially, knees are bent low.
• Distance between two feet: Approximately one and a half or two times the regular stride.
• Techniques preferred: Counterattacking is easily made. Round kicks and backward whip kicks.

■ Stances as related to the opponent

When considering the relationship of competitors stances, there are two possible configurations, open and closed stance.

① Open stance (yŏllimsae)

Open stance suggests that the targets of the head and trunk are open (allowed) to the opponent. Open stance is created when both fighters are in the stance of opposite direction (Ch'ŏng: in a right handed stance, Hong: in a left handed stance).

② Closed Stance (tatch'imsae)

Closed stance suggests that the targets of the opponent are hidden or "closed(tatch'im)" to attacks. This is created when both competitors concurrently assume the stance of the same direction.

(2) Kicks (ch'agi)

Kicks are the essential techniques in Taekwondo competition. Foot techniques are superior to hand techniques in terms of power and the attacking distance.

■ Tips of movements:

• Demonstrate slowly and accurately in the beginning and gradually speed up and repeat.
• Explain the structure, rhythm, flow, and coordination of the movement.
• Explain how to use the physical strength appropriately.
• Slowly learn the movement and practice speedily on a gradual basis.
• Correct the movement and remind the points.

Kicks are a technique of offensive actions using the foot to hit the opponent. Power of kicks comes out of the knee bent and stretched or the moving leg thrown out suddenly.

■ Principles of kicking:

• Increase the concentration of power and the speed of execution to the maximum (concentration and speed)
• Increase speedy and powerful hitting power using the reactive power of the knee or the waist (reaction and power)
• Minimize the time and space toward the target (distance and speed)
• Make the change of the balance of the body to the same direction of the movement (change of balance and direction)

There are various kinds of kicks. The following is the classification of kicks in an order of frequent use during the competition.

■ Tips of training

• Take the exact posture and learn basic kicking techniques correctly.
• Train kicking based on the level of difficulty from basic kicks and technical movements to applied kick and technical movements.
• Enhance the adaptability to real competition by training kicks with training aids or a partner.
• Develop and master special technical movements of one's own.

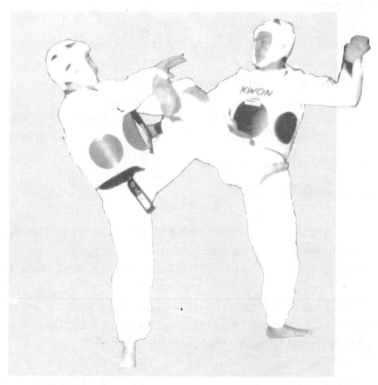

Two players in kyŏrugi at international tournament.

① Round kick (tollyŏ ch'agi)

Chamber the knee and simultaneously pivot 180 degrees on the supporting leg. Using the instep, strike the face or the trunk. This is the most frequently used kick because of its high rate of accuracy and effectiveness.

② Back kick (twi ch'agi)

Pivot on the front foot while chambering the back leg. Quickly look over the turning shoulder at the opponent's movement. Turn the body slightly toward the target while the kicking foot passes by the supporting knee in a direct line to the target. Keep the upper body erect during the execution for maximum efficiency. The target is mainly the trunk. Use the heel and sole of the foot. This is preferred for counterattacking to attacking and has high rate of accuracy. It is effective to execute a long kick in time of attacks and a short kick in time of counterattacks.

③ Backward whip kick (twi huryŏ ch'agi)

Pivot on the front leg and chamber the rear leg. As the body spins around, release the kicking leg in a circular motion. During the spinning movement, quickly look at the opponent over the turning shoulder. Using the sole of the foot, strike the face.

④ Downward kick (naeryŏ ch'agi)

Bend your knee slightly and lift your leg up. As you extend your leg, kick downward. Using the bottom of the foot or heel, strike the face. Depending on the position of your knee, the kick can be executed either with a straight leg or with the knee slightly bent.

⑤ Whip kick (huryŏ ch'agi)

Bring the kicking foot forward and lift the knee. Move the knee forward and bring it around in a circular motion. Using the bottom of the foot, strike the face. The kick can be executed by the front or rear foot.

⑥ Side kick (yŏp ch'agi)

Chamber the leg and thrust it toward the target in a direct linear movement. Using the edge or the heel of the foot, strike the trunk. This is most effective when used as a front leg attack from the side stance.

⑦ Jumping kick (ttwiŏ ch'agi)

All techniques are executed while jumping to the air. Extended time of staying in the air may allow the opponent a chance for counterattack. Try to be as close to the ground as possible when executing the technique in a real competition. This is frequently used as counter offensive actions. It is effective to execute the kick long mainly in attacking and short in counterattacking.

Application
• Jumping back kick (trunk, face)
• Jumping backward whip kick (face)

⑧ Serial kick (iŏ ch'agi)

Execute the technique using one foot for two consecutive times. Different part is used in different techniques. Target area may be different. This is effective when accompanied by high ability and speed to execute techniques.

Application
• Back kick with one foot for two consecutive times
• Backward whip kick and round kick with one foot
• Downward kick and pushing kick with one foot, etc.

⑨ Double kick (tubal tangsŏng)

Jump and perform two kicks consecutively, one with each leg, before landing. Using part of the body and the target differ. This is effective when executed with high performance and speed. Execution of the technique can be made by same or different techniques.

Two kicks may be the same type or different.

Application
• round kick and another round kick (narae ch'agi)

- back kick and a round kick
- round kick and a back kick, etc.

⑩ Pushing kick (mirŏ ch'agi)

The pushing kick is used as a feint or a setup before the main attack. Pushing kick can be executed with the rear leg or the lead leg. Chamber the kicking knee slightly and quickly push toward the waist of the opponent with the sole of the foot.

⑪ Punch (tchirŭgi)

Punching is used as a counterattack or as a tool to create space for follow-up kicks. When the push is accurately and powerfully delivered by the foreknuckles of the fist to the opponent's trunk it can score a point.

⑫ Front kick (ap ch'agi)

This kick is a fundamental in kicking techniques. However, this kick is hardly used in Taekwondo competition.

(3) Footwork / Steps (Chitki)

Footwork or steps "chitki" are a very effective method of attacking and defending as you move your body and shift your balance forward and backward. When you have mastered footwork and stepping, you can blend your footwork from offensive to defensive as well as from defensive to offensive easily. Therefore, footwork are and indirectly but very important part of your sparring.

Depending on the distance and location and body position of your opponent, you choose the proper techniques.

- You can use steps to end or intercept your opponent's attack.
- You could weaken your opponent and find or create the open areas.
- You can find open area as well as time your attack to that area.

■ Tips

There are a few essential points with footwork.

- Move your feet smoothly as if you are sliding over the surface.
- Use agility.
- Shift your balance forward, backward, or sideways depending upon the techniques that you are using.

Footwork is the fundamental technique in Taekwondo competition. You can move in many different directions using these steps: forward, backward, to the side, or turning around. Using these footwork patterns will allow you to maneuver quickly and with great efficiency.

■ Types of Footwork "chitki"

Footwork is an indirect skill used to set up a scoring technique. Footwork changes according to the opponent's stance, position, distance and the situation. The goals of footwork are

1) To disrupt the opponent's offensive strategy
2) To avoid being attacked
3) To create a weakness in the opponent's movements
4) To creates an opening in the opponent's defense
5) To launch an accurate and timely attack

■ Tips for successful footwork

1) Shift the body smoothly and lightly
2) Synchronize the entire body as one unit
3) Maintain equilibrium throughout every movement
4) Adapt the stance according to the technique

① Forward footwork (naga chitki)- depending on the techniques you want to use, the categories are as follows:

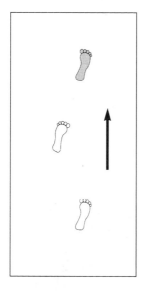 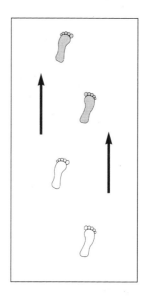

• One foot forward: Quickly step your rear foot forward in front of the front foot and change your sparring position.

• Both foot forward: Maintain foot placement in the sparring stance but shuffle both feet forward. This particular movement is very effective for you to adjust for your attack.

This footwork is best followed by round kick, back kick, and downward kick.

② Backward footwork (mullŏ chitki)

This is almost the opposite of the forward stepping movements. There are two different types of backward steps. The first is moving backward only one step. The second is moving backward further using two steps.

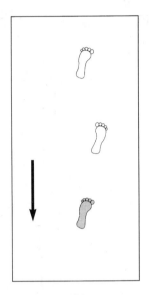
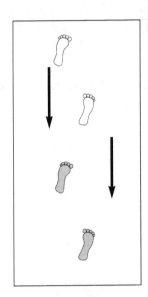

• One foot backward: Move the front foot back to the rear foot and then move the rear foot backwards. Your stance should not change. If the left foot was forward, at the end of this step, the left foot is still forward.

• Both foot backward: Move the front foot back to the rear foot and then move the rear foot backwards. Your stance should not change. If the left foot was forward, the left foot is still forward at the end of this step.

This footwork is best followed by round kick, back kick, and spin whip kick.

③ Lateral footwork (pikkyŏ chitki)

Move either front or rear foot to the side or both feet to the side.

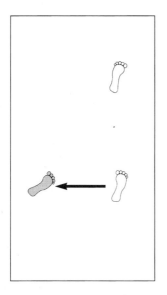
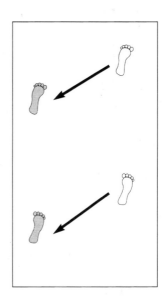

• One foot laterally: Pick up the rear foot and move it 45 degrees sideways leaving the front foot stationary.
• Both feet laterally: Move your front foot to either side at a 45 degree angle and follow up with the rear foot.

This footwork is best followed by round kick, downward kick, and back spin kick.

④ Turning backward footwork (twidora chitki)

Keeping the front foot stationary, pick up the rear foot and pivot on the front foot. Turn your body to the backside while pivoting and step forward with the rear foot.

This footwork is best followed by round kick, downward kick, and whip kick.

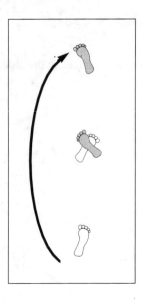

⑤ Drawing footwork (kullŏ chitki)

Bring the front foot back to the rear foot and immediately step forward with the rear foot. You can also step the rear foot up to the front foot and bring the front foot back to where the rear foot position was.

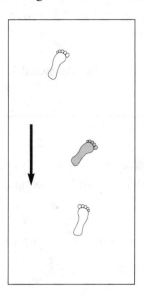

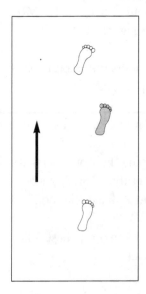

This footwork is best followed by round kick, downward kick, and whip kick.

■ Method of practice

There are several guidelines and ways to practice these techniques.
• Form correct posture and understand the formats of the stepping and footwork movements.
• Move your feet smoothly and accurately.
• Practice timing of these techniques by following the tojang leader's command.
• Develop endurance, agility, and speed as you practice.

As stated above, the following suggestions are effective in developing speed and flexibility in stepping maneuvers. Speed and flexibility are two of the most important aspects of these footwork drills.

① First stage: Stepping practice

Practice these stepping movements repeatedly. These footwork patterns should be automatic responses or habits and should be executed smoothly.

We suggest not to use kicks while learning and practice these various stepping movements. Focus on the footwork only until it become natural and you develop proper form.

Follow the tojang leader's direction and practice in front of a minor. That way you can see and critique your own movements much like Taekwondo practitioners do in working on P'umsae.

Developing your flexibility and elasticity through this training is essential. You should be flexible to adapt and use any or all of these stepping movements quickly and smoothly. In order to have automatic responses with footwork, your body needs to be flexible to perform at its maximum potential.

② Second stage

Now practice the steps with a partner. Continually drilling these footwork movements will develop rhythm and speed. As you practice the steps, pay close attention to the timing of your techniques. Be aware of the rhythm and timing of your opponent and visualize his/her responses.

③ Third stage: Stepping Kick Practice

Do not begin adding kicks to these movements until you feel you have developed proper form, rhythm, and speed. When you do add kicking techniques to these steps, you will develop total muscle strength throughout your body.

④ Fourth stage

Do the steps with Kyŏrugi practice using your kicks as if you are really sparring. That means that you can practice attacking, counterattacking, counterkicking along with the forms and timing of the steps. The main focus of this training is your timing, speed, agility, and control so that you can develop your overall sparring ability.

Taekwondo matches require 3 rounds each lasting 3 minutes in time. We suggest that you practice 3-5 sets of these 3 rounds. This will develop overall endurance.

(4) Covering

In Taekwondo, blocking is a very important skill to acquire. We can divide blocking techniques into 2 separate categories: direct and indirect blocking.

Direct blocking: Mainly use your forearm or hand to block the opponent's punch or kick.

Indirect blocking: Distance yourself and avoid your opponent's attack by backing up or side stepping. Another indirect blocking method is to position your arms or legs in the expected target area so that your opponent cannot attack that area. You must quickly cover the target area in order to prevent the attack or weaken the attack.

There are many different variations of covering depending on where the attack is intended and your quick response to the attack. You must be able to position your arms so that you can efficiently cover the area and adapt to a new position.

The main areas to cover are the face and the trunk, especially the front and both sides of the trunk.

As prerequisites for that purpose, basic techniques should be performed in the following ways:

■ Methods of Covering

• Cover the expected area that your opponent is intending to attack.
• Make your movements more efficient. Improve your covering ability.
• Your sparring stance should allow you to use both arms in a position where you can block any area on your body.

■ Tips

• Face and trunk (sides of the trunk)

Use one arm to cover the face and the other to cover the body when your opponent uses continual or multiple attacks to the face and body.

• Front of the trunk

If your opponent attacks your torso only, bring your arms closer to your body and cover the lower area.

• Both sides of the trunk

When your opponent attacks the sides of your torso, use your elbows to cover the areas.

These methods are useful in competition for covering when your opponent attacks you with speed. However, during training, we encourage you to develop more blocking skills than just these covering techniques. In competition, actual blocking has not been used as effective as covering. But blocking techniques remain a very valuable tool.

(5) Deceptive Movements (Feint)

Deceptive movements are used very frequently in Taekwondo competition as tactical techniques.

■ Purpose of feinting

  • Creates an open area in your opponent's defense.
  • Neutralize or disrupt your opponent's attacking tactics.

■ Tips

  • Use of bodily gestures and the foot: You move the upper body or make a chitki in order to induce the opponent to expose his vulnerable a points before you seize the opportunity to deliver an attack.

  Feint motions of attack: You make a feint motion as if you are willing to attack in order to invite a change in the opponent's movements before you seize chance to attack.

  Inducement of the opponent's attack: You keep your own attack areas open to induce the opponent to deliver an attack.

Factors of Taekwondo Techniques

Sŏgi (Stance)

State of the foot	State of the foot	Relativity with opponent
Orŭn Kyŏrumse	Orŭn Kyŏrumse	Yŏllimse
Oen Kyŏrumse	Oen Kyŏrumse	Tach'imse

Ch'agi, Tchirŭgi

- tollyŏ ch'agi
- twi ch'agi
- twi huryŏ ch'agi
- naeryŏ ch'agi
- huryŏ ch'agi
- yŏp ch'agi
- ap ch'agi
- (momt'ong) tchirŭgi

Chitgi

- naga chitgi
- mullŏ chitgi
- pikkyo chitgi
- twidora chitgi
- kkŭro chitgi

Makki

- direct makki
- indirect makki

Chapter 3 THREE

Tactical and Technical Practice

Tactical and technical practice or exercise means that the competitor trains to achieve maturity in mental tactics and execution of the physical techniques in competition.

Practicing these aspects of training allows the competitor to use them effectively in actual competition. Practice means to improve your techniques as well as the tactical aspects of your performance. This means that you develop the best execution of these techniques efficiently.

① Favorite Special Techniques

Diligently practicing special techniques allows the competitors to use them very effectively when sparring.

There are two basic steps in practicing special techniques:

• Consistent practice of the techniques thereby obtaining the skill and ability to call it your own.
• Once you obtain the techniques, improve or mature them so that you can execute them quickly, easily, and effectively.

■ Practicing guidelines

• Practice these techniques throughout your entire training period.
• Practice with high numbers of repetition.
• Focus on accuracy, agility, and efficient speed.
• Have positive intention and coordination and powerful concentration.

■ Drills using tollyŏ ch'agi (round kick to the trunk and the face)

• Twi tollyŏ ch'agi in the standing position
• Two feet continuous tollyŏ ch'agi (round kick)
• One foot back up tollyŏ ch'agi (round kick)

• One foot step forward and execute rear foot tollyŏ ch'agi (round kick)
  • Twi tollyŏ ch'agi (backward round kick)
  • Pull front foot back tollyŏ ch'agi (round kick)
  • Both feet pull back tollyŏ ch'agi (round kick)

■ Drills using twi ch'agi (back kick to the trunk)

• Standing straight twi ch'agi (back kick)
• Front foot step forward twi ch'agi (back kick)
• Rear foot step forward ttwio twi ch'agi (back kick)
• One foot full back twi ch'agi (back kick)
• Both feet full back twi ch'agi (back kick)

■ Drills using naeryŏ ch'agi (downward kick to the face)

• One foot naeryŏ ch'agi (downward kick)
• Jump and front foot naeryŏ ch'agi (downward kick)
• One foot pull back naeryŏ ch'agi (downward kick)
• Both feet pull back naeryŏ ch'agi (downward kick)

■ Drills using twi huryŏ ch'agi (backward whip kick to the face)

• Standing twi huryŏ ch'agi (backward whip kick)
• One step forward twi huryŏ ch'agi (backward whip kick)
• One step backward twi huryŏ ch'agi (backward whip kick)
• Both feet pull back twi huryŏ ch'agi (backward whip kick)

2

Practice with a Partner

When you drill with a partner, use limited techniques and have a more realistic mind set and active performance. One of the most important drills that your partner can do for you is to repeatedly attack with one or two techniques.

This will allow you to become comfortable with that particular attack and your response will be quicker and more effective. Your partner's reaction or resistance may vary tremendously. Therefore, practice and drill with great concentration using accurate and well placed techniques.

Practicing with a partner to improve your competition sparring may be divided into two different categories:

• Practice using both feet to maintain balance between your left and right side in executing techniques. Focus on improving your ability to judge timing, accuracy, and distance with your partner.

• Practice all these techniques varying your sparring stance. This will give you a variety of styles and approaches for you to use.

■ Methods of practice

In general, this is done with two people making one team. Tactical and technical components to be used are predetermined. Contestants should focus on the execution of technically accurate movements.

• Stationary
• Forward footwork
• Backward footwork
• Lateral footwork (both sides)

Practice with different partners if possible to improve your adaptability.

• Attacking and counterattacking
• Use various techniques using stepping footwork patterns
• Use sparring aids and equipment (hogu, targets, etc.)

■ Application

• You could use these drills with a leader giving a verbal command or hand signal.
• Feint stepping in free sparring practice
• Practice focusing on speed and agility
• Drill quickly and rapidly to improve your endurance and stamina

■ Technical points of practice (A is attacker, B is counterattacker)

A- in open fighting stance executing tollyŏ ch'agi to B's trunk
B- covers trunk with both arms while executing counter punch

A- in open stance executes tollyŏ ch'agi to B's trunk
B- quickly counters with back foot twi ch'agi

A- in closed fighting stance tollyŏ ch'agi towards the trunk
B- uses front arm covering trunk and counters with rear hand punch

A- in closed stance attacks with tollyŏ ch'agi to the face

B- uses front arm covering face while leaning slightly backwards and executes rear foot tollyŏ ch'agi to A's trunk

A- in closed stance uses rear foot twi huryŏ ch'agi

B- uses front foot tollyŏ ch'agi to A's upper trunk

A- in closed stance attacks with naeryŏ ch'agi to B's body

B- steps back and immediately uses rear foot tollyŏ ch'agi

3

Tactical Exercise of Techniques

This method uses two or more techniques in combination to attack your opponent. Repeated practice improves and perfects your techniques while tactically developing a good sense of timing, adaptability, and proper execution in competition.

■ Tactical Styles of Practice

- Without hogu (protective equipment)
- With hogu
- Using other training aids (targets)

When drilling without hogu, you should focus on developing your control, accuracy, speed, and timing to improve your technical execution and perfection. When using hogu, your focus should be to use the techniques that can score in competition. Developing power, timing, getting the feel of wearing the hogu is necessary in competition. Practicing with training aids allows you to develop your accuracy, power, and quickening your counter kicks.

In general, when practicing with a partner, your sparring position could be closed or opened as it is in real competition. With both these stances, use the steps and footwork patterns and counterattacking techniques in practice. Stances can shift from open to closed. So you need to be able to adapt to your opponent's position. This drill requires a great deal of experience because your opponent is not in a fixed position.

■ Types of Practice

• Closed or open fighting stance use two or more combined techniques (initiate attacking)
• Feint and attack depending on your opponent's response
• Attacking and counterattacking — in most technical execution, one initiates attack and the other counterattacks.

(1) In closed fighting stance

Attacking Styles

① Rear foot drawing footwork and front foot round kick to the trunk or the face

• Maintain the proper distance to initiate attack.
• When you execute the kick, minimize the distance and timing of the attack.
• Cover your body in case your opponent counterkicks.

② Rear foot drawing footwork and front foot downward kick to the face

• Maintain the same sparring stance.
• Bend your knee of the kicking foot. Raise the leg and extend to kick to the face.
• This is effective when your opponent does not back or attempts to do close in fighting.

③ Triple round kicks to the trunk

• Use the rear foot to kick and follow up with two consecutive round

kicks either left, right or right, left.
- This technique takes tremendous skill, speed and coordination.
- When executing, bend your upper body slightly backward.

④ Jumping backward round kick to the face or the trunk

- Requires rapid turning of your body.
- Focus on the target area of your opponent.
- While you are executing, make sure your arms are covering your body.

⑤ Back kick

- This is a linear kick.
- Maintain your body in a vertical position.
- Use your waist to generate your turning power.

⑥ Front foot lateral footwork and front foot round kick to the face or the trunk

- Step the front foot to the side and move the rear foot one step forward.
- Execute a short round kick.
- Requires rapid footwork.

⑦ Front foot lateral footwork and downward kick.

- Step the front foot to the side and move the rear foot forward.
- Execute a front foot axe kick in a semi-circular manner.
- This technique is good for close fighting.
- Requires quick movement and rapid execution while you are moving your body.

⑧ Double round kick

- Execute a short rear foot round kick and immediately follow up with another round with the other foot.

• Draw power from the kicking foot to follow up with the consecutive kick. Short rapid movement is required.

⑨ Change the stance and round kick

• From a closed stance, switch your feet to an open stance.
• Immediately kick or respond based on how your opponent reacts to your change in stance.
• This requires much agility.

⑩ Front foot feint and jump back kick

• Use front foot feint.
• Immediately kick depending on how your opponent reacts to the feint.

⑪ Front foot feint and front foot round kick to the face

• Use the front foot feint motion and follow up with a quick, short, reflexive kick.

⑫ Rear foot feint motion followed by the jump downward kick with the front foot

⑬ Rear foot feint motion and bring the rear foot forward executing the double consecutive round kicks (tubal tangsŏng)

⑭ Front foot feint, rear foot step up and front foot round kick to the face

⑮ Front foot feint motion, rear foot side footwork and immediately follow up with a jump kick

⑯ Front foot feint motion, jump back whip kick by the rear foot drawing footwork

⑰ Front foot feint motion, step the rear foot up and execute a round kick with the rear foot

⑱ Either front or rear foot feint, step forward and execute a round kick

⑲ Back kick feint motion, turn around and follow up with a turning back round kick

Counterattacking Styles

• Bring your rear foot to the front and use your front foot to deliver a round kick.
• Bring your rear foot backward followed by the front foot, round kick.
• Countering against jumping kicks.
• Bring front foot backward, and round kick.
• Both feet backwards footwork, and execute a double round kicks (left, right or right, left)
• Bring front foot to the rear and front foot round kick to the face.
• Bring both feet backward can turn executing a jumping round kick to the trunk.
• Front foot side footwork and execute a front hand punch followed by front foot round kick.
• Front foot side footwork and execute a front hand punch followed by front foot whip kick.

① Countering against rear foot round to the trunk:

• Both feet step backwards and rear foot round kick to the trunk.
• Front foot stepping and rear foot whip kick.
• Front foot step back to the rear foot and execute a jump round kick to the trunk with the rear foot.
• Rear hand punch and rear foot round kick.
• Rear hand punch and rear foot whip kick.

② Countering against rear foot whip kick:

- Rear foot back step and execute a rear foot round kick to the trunk.
- Front foot pull back and rear foot round kick.
- Front foot push kick forward and follow up with rear foot back kick.

③ Countering against front foot jumping whip kick:

- Rear foot back up and front foot pull back and round kick.
- Stationary front foot round kick.
- Jump back whip kick.
- Front foot back footwork and round kick.

④ Countering against front foot push kick:

- In stationary position, front foot round kick.
- Front foot pull back and round kick.

⑤ Countering against a rear foot back kick:

- Both feet backward footwork and rear foot round kick.
- Front foot backward footwork and back kick.
- Front foot lateral step and round kick.

⑥ Countering against the rear foot whip kick:

- In stationary position, front foot pushing kick.
- In stationary position, round kick.
- In stationary position, rear foot back whip kick.
- Both feet step backward and round kick.
- One foot step backward and round kick.
- One foot step backward and push kick.

⑦ Countering against a jumping turning backward round kick:

- Rear foot round kick.
- Jump back kick.
- Rear whip kick.
- Front foot pull back and whip kick.
- Both feet pull back and consecutive round kicks. (tubal tangsŏng ch'agi)

⑧ Counterattacking against an opponent who continuously changes sparring position and attacks with round kicks:

- Front foot whip kick.
- Jumping back kick.
- Round kick.

⑨ In a closed stance, switch to an open stance when your opponent attacks with a rear foot back kick:

- Both feet step backward, rear foot round kick.
- Both feet step backward, double round kick.
- Rear foot whip kick.

(2) In open fighting stance

Counterattacking methods

Now we will cover methods of counterattacking and counterattacking from an open stance.

① Attacking methods:

- Rear foot round to the trunk.
- Rear foot round to the face.
- Rear foot whip kick.
- Rear foot double round with the same foot.

• One foot step backward, back kick and follow up with consecutive round kicks.

② Counterattacking methods:

• Counterkicking against rear foot round.
• Front foot pull back, round kick.
• Jumping back kick.
• Back whip kick.
• Both feet step backward, follow up with consecutive round kicks.
• Front foot round kick to the face.
• Front foot side step and round kick.
• Stationary rear foot back kick.
• Stationary rear foot whip kick. (Pull your front foot slightly backwards)
• Both feet step back, backward round kick.

③ Counterkicking against rear foot downward kick:

• Both feet step back, front foot round kick.
• Back kick.
• Back whip kick.
• Both feet side step, round kick.
• Stationary jumping kick.
• Stationary rear foot jumping back kick.
• Stationary front foot round kick. (Bend your trunk slightly backwards)
• Both feet step back, rear foot whip kick.
• Both feet step back, jumping back kick.

④ Counterattacking in closed position:

• Both feet step back, back whip kick.
• Both feet step back, round kick.
• Front foot side step, round kick.

4

Exercise with the Training Aids

■ Drilling with training aids and equipment

To improve your competition sparring ability, there are many different training aids to use. The most frequently used aids are targets and focus mitts, jump rope. Hogu is the protective equipment that competitors must wear during competition matches. But it can also be used as a target for drilling purposes. It is advisable to wear hogu when training so that you get used to wearing it for competition and become familiar with how it feels. Targets and mitts are excellent training tools for drilling. They are versatile because they can be used as a stationary or moving target for the competitor to practice kicks and punches.

(1) Targets and mitts

These training aids help in improving accuracy, agility, concentration, and focus. When used as movable targets, they especially help to improve reflexes and speed.

＊ Note — Speed, accuracy, and the quickness of your response are very important factors in competition. Become familiar with noticing the distance to the targets and select the appropriate technique to execute. Combining your judgement of distance and attacking technique with stepping footwork will create the desired results. Competitors must be familiar with judging distance and executing the proper techniques.

■ Methods of holding

Hold the target and stand comfortably in front of your partner. Hold the target firmly and keep the elbow slightly bent. Extend your arm forward and adjust the distance to your partner depending on what technique you are drilling.

① Basic kick: Most basic kicks (and punches) are to hit squarely on target to improve its efficiency. This method involves two people to a team. The team can work independently or with a leader's command.

② Moving front and back kicking drills: This method is very helpful for competition training. Holder moves backwards and forwards with the target. The partner must adjust the distance and execute the techniques quickly. This helps to develop accuracy, timing, and agility.

③ Footwork kick: Depending on the target holder's position, the kicker can use various stepping footwork patterns to approach the target holder and execute the techniques. While you are moving, focus on flexibility, adaptability, quick responses, and agility. These areas are very important for a competitor. Agility in kicking needs to be developed so that you have power and control in the kicks.

④ Reflex kick: Target holder holds the target behind his/her body. Use a quick visual or auditory cue, and at the same time bring the target forward. The attacker must quickly choose the appropriate technique to use depending on the distance and placement of the target. This develops quick reflexes, speed, and timing in addition to improving the kicker's quick selection of which technique to use. This training requires a high amount of concentration. When you feel fatigued, stop this drill. We suggest for your daily training schedule that you do this drill in the first half of the training session so as not to be too fatigued before this drill.

⑤ Shuttle kick: Use two holders and maintaining proper distance to the kicker. A helper stands in the middle of the two target holders. The kicker's response is based on the helper's visual or auditory cue and direction. The important part of this training is to improve the execution and ability of movement. You can gauge your improvement by checking the number of kicks executed and compare it with another group to create a competitive spirit. This will improve speed, control, and flexibility.

⑥ Kyŏrugi kick: Holder moves around freely in any direction. This method is very useful for improvement of timing and control. Use three round, each three minutes in length.

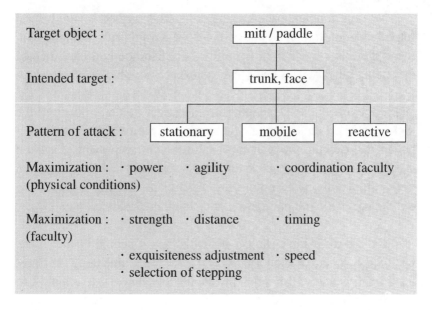

Target object :		mitt / paddle	
Intended target :		trunk, face	
Pattern of attack :	stationary	mobile	reactive

Maximization :   · power   · agility   · coordination faculty
(physical conditions)

Maximization :   · strength   · distance   · timing
(faculty)

            · exquisiteness adjustment   · speed
            · selection of stepping

(2) Jump ropes

Jump ropes are very good training aids that greatly improve overall body conditioning. They do not require much space so they are an ideal training aid. Skipping rope should be adjusted based on competitor's level.

• Maintain a firm upper body. Keep your eyes straight forward.
• Relax your shoulders and arms and hold your arms in close to your body.
• Maintain your abdominal area and concentrate on breathing regularly.
• Relax your wrists and hold them at waist level moving them in a controlled and circular motion.
• Bend your knee slightly and use the ball of your foot when you are jumping.
• There are many different methods of skipping rope: both feet together, one foot, switch feet, changing direction, moving back and forth.
• Jump and kick knee height, double skipping, etc.

■ Methods

• 2 minutes, 6 times — Change your speed during the rounds and allow a one minute rest.
• 3 minutes, 3 times — Increase your speed during the rounds and allow a one minute rest.

■ Effect

• Skipping rope improves lung capacity and agility, flexibility, and balance.
• Skipping rope for 10 minutes is equivalent to 30 minutes' jogging.
• In addition to the training aids mentioned before, you could use heavy punching bags, air shields, weight jackets, and or wrist and ankle bands.

Chapter 4 FOUR

Condition

Physical Stamina (Condition)

Condition is the basis of all human capabilities in bodily action. In other words, conditioning determines all bodily functions; how well one can carry on. Conditioning is related to the health of the person and directly related to the performance of the competitor. Conditioning, or sports conditioning, deals with the muscles, endurance, and control.

These three combined factors help to promote bodily capacity to help perform and achieve certain goals in competition. Taekwondo conditioning requires a balanced body with a high level of physical fitness.

(1) Muscular Strength and Power

Power, or force, is the changing of an object's direction or movement. In sports, force means muscular strength as well as power. Force means the strength occurs in an action containing speed. Muscular strength means static, or stationary. Muscular strength is stationary; or static, when it creates power.

Power means, in competition that the muscle can create an explosive strength or force. This means that we can define it in terms of kinetic concepts. This also means that it's necessary to condition movement in an active sense. In other words, actively pursuing to perform certain movements. Power, or strength of power determines the muscle and the speed.

In Taekwondo, we need strong muscular strength which can be developed by weight training. In order for us to punch well, we need to develop muscles in our arms, back, and chest; in kicking, abdominal muscles and legs.

Muscular strength is directly related to the size of the cross section of the muscle. All movement is carried on by the human body by muscles that are attached to the muscles by joints by a relaxing and contradicting movement. Every movement we do is due to the relaxation and contractions of the muscles attached to the joints.

■ Muscular Strength

  • Thigh Power
  • Upper Body Strength
  • Stomach Strength

■ Condition of Training

  • Strengthening muscular strength: Whole or local muscles training (weight training), resistance training, static training (isometric weight training)

■ Necessary for better Taekwondo kicks

  • Flying split
  • Jumping split
  • Full squats barbells
  • Single leg squat
  • Leg curls, etc.

■ Strengthening to increase speed

- Maximum capacity of 80% or higher
- Heavy weight equipment training (weight-loading belt, sandbags, etc., either on ankle or on wrist)
  - Kicks using Taekwondo training aid like target or mitt
  - Climbing the stairs or slope at a full speed
  - Stationary jumping (15-20 times)
  - Stationary jumping & kicking (15-20 times)

(2) Speed and Agility

Speed is a major factor in movement and also promotes the human body to promote the human body to provide a quick movement capacity. Speed reflects the human body's quick performances;

- The same continual movement or execution of the same size, shape, and speed (Barrow & McGee, 1966)
- The entire bodily movement from one position to another (Updike & Johnson, 1970)
- Part of the speed of the body's movement (Fleishman, 1964)

As listed above, the researcher's definition of speed is using the arms and legs to the capacity or ability of movement without having accuracy, skills or strength.

Agility is the ability to change direction effectively with maximum speed from one position to another (Updike & Johnson, 1970).

Agility is to muscle strength, speed of response, power, coordination, and flexibility. Agility is also determined by the speed of the relaxation and contractions, which in turn is related to the speed of the reflex by the central nervous system.

In Taekwondo competition, this agility is a decisive factor in executing techniques. In all, or every defensive/offensive action, agility is determined by this quickness combined with other complex issues. Reflexes are the issues of Taekwondo competition. During competition, the competitor should be sensitive and aware of his opponent who is constantly moving, and at the same time, and be able to provide active, reflexive reactions (kick, counterkick, footwork, etc.). The competitor must be able to execute these crucial techniques.

In order for one to improve his speed, the following issues must be resolved.

• Explosive powers
• All available explicit powers must be mobilized and strengthened; or strengthening mobility in terms of explosive power. All training is precisely related to techniques. All speed training must be related and connected to technical training.

If you want to do special training to improve your speed, the following two conditions are advised to be kept.

• Training using targets or mitt: Training must be conducted only with self-improvement of Taekwondo techniques. If and when while executing techniques you spot a faulty movement, stop training with that method immediately.

• Training using weight on either arms or legs: In order to improve speed of muscular strength, frequency of movement must be raised and weight loading training must be repeated.

You can expect to have the effect of weight load if and when the techniques in competition are in accordance with the structure of movement. All of the Taekwondo techniques must be accompanied in maximum speed. Resting intervals are essential for maximum performance. Make sure you take plenty of rest so that you can be fully recovered. If you feel any signs or symptoms of fatigue, stop and take a rest. Fatigue will lower the speed of your performance and concentration.

■ Method of training

• 25 to 30 meter sprints, full speed 7 to 10 meters (3 sets)
• Skipping (stationary, knee kicks to chest)
• Explosive kicking techniques or stepping (side, forward, back)
• Run 20 meters 3 times in a zigzag
• Jump rope (compete who can do the most repetitions in one
minute)
• Quick change in direction based on audio-visual signals (sitting,
standing up, running, etc.)

(3) Endurance

Endurance is the ability of the whole body to continue an exercise for
a set duration of time. In order to maintain overall endurance, you need
to control breathing, circular motion, and continually supply oxygen to
your body. Taekwondo requires a continual improvement of endurance.
In particular, Taekwondo competition is an aerobic exercise. During
Taekwondo training, basic endurance must be developed. In
competition, special professional types of endurance must be
developed. Training should be aerobic conditioning under the area of
the conditioning that you should execute your performance. Aerobic
training means that fatigue must be delayed, which usually occurs two
minutes after an exercise starts.

The period of exercise should be extended to raise the ability to create
energies by muscles and intensity of exercise should be also raised to
improve the system to deliver oxygen through the blood stream.

In training for endurance, the amount of the load should be selected
according to the condition. In general, it is effective to train to make the
heart beat to be 140 to 170 times a minute.

■ Methods of training

① Basic endurance

• Long distance running (1,000m × 3 times with one minute rest inbetween)
• Interval running (100m × 5 times with one minute rest inbetween)

② Professional endurance

• Repeated sparring exercise (three rounds of three minutes each with one minute rest inbetween)
• Stair running (8 to 10 items to be designated)
• Pitching (jumping in place with alternative knee raises by 90 degrees, 50 times × 3 sets)
• Target kicking
• Circuit training (select Taekwondo related disciplines)

(4) Flexibility

Flexibility is the general elasticity of the ligaments in dynamic and stationary conditions, including the availability of the joints and the elasticity of the muscles. Flexibility, an important factor to determine the range of the motion, is closely related to the coordination ability. It is a fundamental prerequisite of the sporting ability in Taekwondo. Raised flexibility enables and improves dodging, kicking and adjusting the distance more rapidly during a particular motion. In Taekwondo training, it is important to develop good flexibility in the shoulders, waists (hip joints), knees and ankles. Sufficient warming up is needed to prevent injuries in training to raise the flexibility.

Flexibility can be raised by calisthenics which increases oxygen supply and heart beat, thus maximizing the supply of oxygen and blood to the muscles. It is desirable to conduct calisthenics every day with 20 to 30 minutes at once. Stretching is also widely known as a method to enhance the flexibility. Stretching stretches muscles and tendons of every part of the body to enable physiological effect to improve the general muscles and tendons. Stretching is widely used as a warming up and a winding up. In Taekwondo, it is effective to do stretching after fully understanding the muscles and tendons frequently used in Taekwondo. Stretching should be repeatedly done in a stationary period for 10 to 20 seconds at least three to five times with concentration of the mind on the pertinent muscles.

■ Effects

- Explosive attacking power
- Motion taken in a wide amplitude
- Reduction in possibilities of injuries

■ Drilling methods

- Individual stretching: stretching done alone
- Passive stretching: two athletes cooperate with each other to stretch the muscles and tendons of the partner. This is more effective than the one done alone.
- Perfect motion (exercise) by performing a technique

■ Tips

- Frequency: done every day or two times a day
- Stretch until you feel a slight pain
- Stretching is effective after warming up or the main training
- Stretch for about 10 to 15 minutes at the room temperature
- Fully stretch muscles and tendons frequently used in Taekwondo

Stretching has no direct effect on strengthening the muscle power. However, it helps to develop the muscle power when accompanied by the isometric (same-size contraction) exercises.

■ Methods of Stretching

① Outside of the thigh

• Stand upright and lean one hand to a wall or something to keep the stance.
• Take one ankle with the other hand and slowly raise the ankle and stretch the front of the thigh.

② Inside of the thigh

• Put one foot on the waist-high desk or something.
• Bend your upper body until your chin contacts the knee and stretch the inner part of the thigh. (Be careful not to make the knee bent.)

③ Calves

• Put both hands onto the wall with one foot forward.
• Fully stretch the calf of the back leg as if you lean your body forward. (Do not load your weight on the front leg if possible. Don't pull your elbow and composedly perform the motion to sustain the body.)

④ Lower parts of calves

• Put both hands onto the wall with one foot forward.
• Bend the knee of the back leg and stretch the calf. (Do not pull the knee and composedly perform the motion to sustain the body.)

⑤ Inner parts of arms and armpits

• Raise both arms over the head and bend the elbow.
• Take the left elbow with the right hand.
• Pull the elbow and turn the waist aside and stretch the inner part of
the arm and the armpit. (Be careful to load the weight to both hands
evenly.)

⑥ Waist, abdomen, back

• Stand against the wall.
• Turn the upper body and put both hands onto the wall and stretch the waist, the abdomen and the back. (Don't turn the waist if possible.)

⑦ Shoulders

• Stretch the left elbow and make the left at level.
• Take the levelled arm with the right hand.
• Pull the levelled arm as close to the chest as possible and stretch the shoulder.

⑧ Head

• Raise the left hand over the head.
• Turn the head aside using the weight of the bent arm. (Be careful not to pull the arm excessively.)
• Get the fingers crossed in the back of the head. Bend the head forward and stretch the head using the weight of the arms. (Do not press the head excessively.)

(5) Coordination

Coordination is the ability to quickly and accurately respond to the constantly changing opponent's movements. Coordination is a prerequisite to the execution of a motion and the ability of a combined response. It helps to learn skills easily and perfectly and adapt them as necessary in variable situations. Coordination is closely related to such factors of physical strength as accuracy, balance, timing, flexibility, and agility.

In Taekwondo, following abilities can be achieved by coordination training:

① Responsiveness

Responsiveness is the ability to react quickly and appropriately to expected or unexpected sensory cues. This is developed by training most close to the real competition. Responsiveness is the physical reflex drills to the opponent's movements and kicking techniques.

Drilling methods
- Responsive drills (mainly visual ones)
- Psychological drills (concentration of mind, activeness)

Examples
- Kicks and counterkicks
- Responses to the opponent's tactics

② Analysis

Analysis is to discern the physical conditions of the opponent in visual, auditory, reactive, and tactical forms. It is an ability to accurately observe and evaluate the opponent's reactions.

Examples
- Observe and evaluate the opponent quickly and accurately.

- Discern the opponent's reactions.
- Analyze the situation of himself/herself and the opponent in the competition area.

③ Extrapolation

Extrapolation is the ability to forecast his/her or the opponent's technical or tactical behavior based on experience of competitions and special actions in a distance of available attacks in competitions.

Examples
- Set up the behavior or estimate the opponent's response with obvious technical and tactical attitudes.
- Feint the opponent intentionally, etc.

④ Integration

Behaviors especially required in Taekwondo are dependent on the constantly changing situation in the competition arena. Prerequisites of the tactically right response to the situation are the accuracy of the motion, distance, the ability to perform, and adaption to the situation. This is accomplished by coordination of total body movements with movements of the individual arms and legs. This actually takes a great part of basic training in Taekwondo.

Examples
- Footwork
- Trunk movements (vertical, horizontal or spinning)
- Arm vibration and movement (reaction)
- Foot kicking movement (movement ring, upward and downward withdrawal, foot kicks)

⑤ Transformation

Transformation is the ability to manipulate physical techniques and tactical considerations to take advantage of an unfavorable situation.

Examples
- Transformation from being set up by the opponent's feint.
- Transformation from failing to predict the opponent's reaction.
- Transformation from attacking with the wrong technique.
- Transformation from unfavorable external environment (ex: poor competition floor, unfavorable spectators, unfavorable conditions of games hall) and internal emotional turmoil (nervousness, insecurity, passivity, arrogance)

⑥ Differentiation

Differentiation is the ability to execute accurate and versatile techniques in a motion, process of a motion or a series of motions.

- Strengthening kicking techniques based on accurate kicks, maturity, and power appropriate to a situation.
- This ability is achieved by changes of execution in a distance and speed appropriate to a strategic situation of a competition.

⑦ Timing

Timing is the ability to select the best time, speed, rhythm or tempo for performing the proper technique so as to achieve the desired result. An excellent Taekwondo athlete is the one who can select the best time, speed, stance, location and technique in a situation.

It is important in Taekwondo competition for synchronizing and harmonizing the entire body actions and executing scoring techniques.

Timing ability can be measured through reflex time and execution time. It can be improved through practice but it is an innate skill.

Right timing enhances the possibility of scoring and can be developed through practice, sparring exercises, and real competitions. Sporting ability can be improved by timing drills.

Examples
- Flexibility, coordination
- Tactical thinking
- Tactical attacking
- Rhythm and tempo

Training for Conditioning

Physical strength is the physical and mental ability to execute bodily activities in life. It is the combination of mental strength and physical power. It involves wisdom, emotion, and general factors of physical strength. Taekwondo is an exercise of the whole body. Taekwondo competition requires physical power for action which increases the use of active exercise organs.

Training is a process which strengthen the factors of physical power. Training is reversible and its effect diminishes if we stop training. But practice has a long lasting effect. This training is aimed at strengthening physical abilities or functions and making our body fit for high techniques using high human adaptability and based on scientifically reasonable training method, thus improving the game's result. Physical strength is divided into basic strength and professional strength. Basic physical strength is the factors of physical strength like agility, speed, power, balance, flexibility, coordination and muscular strength. Professional physical strength needed in Taekwondo includes power, flexibility, and coordination which is the combination of extrapolation and responsiveness.

(1) Weight Training

Weight training is a training to load weight to strengthen muscular strength. This is the most commonly used training method for developing muscular strength. This training is aimed at developing and strengthenining mainly muscular strength, muscular endurance and power.

Athletes have to develop professional physical strength or to do supplemental training during the off season. Taekwondo athletes have to strengthen muscles of the legs and the waist in particular. Weight training can be conducted in a way to combine similar forms of movements to kicking techniques.

This training requires exact stances and right respiration method. Its general principles are as follows.

• Gradually develop, increase and strengthen muscular strength through appropriate load training and resistance load training under the principle of gradual overload.
• Contraction of the muscles which generates power is called dynamic contraction. Taekwondo techniques are executed mainly through this kind of contraction.

■ Method

  • Set and repetition: 3-4 sets, 8-10 times
  • Frequency: 1-3 times a week
  • Intensity: 60-70% of the maximum capacity

■ Effect

Improve muscular strength, muscular endurance and power

- Kinds

  - Sit up
  - Bend over
  - Full squat
  - Leg extension
  - Leg curl
  - Leg press
  - Deep knee bend
  - Bench press
  - Crucifix

(2) Circuit Training

Circuit training is an overall physical strength training. This is a kind of physical strength training and strengthening training. This is a training to gradually strengthen muscular strength and power. This is aimed at strengthening the function of respiratory organs.

One set consists of at least 8-12 kinds which are implemented in order. No rest between the kinds in a set or between the sets makes this training effective to the whole body including muscular, respiratory, nervous and bone systems.

- Method

  - Set and repetition: 6-10 sets, 20-30 times
  - Frequency: 3 times a week, or every other day
  - Time of training: 15-30 minutes

- Effect

Improve muscular strength, power and speed

■ Kinds

- Push up
- Trunk curl
- Full squat
- Squat jump
- Straddle jump
- Squat thrust
- Burpee
- Jumping
- High jump
- Side stepping
- Trunk backward extension
- Sit up

(3) Interval Training

Interval training is the training to increase the endurance of the whole body. Short training is repeated with the rest being dynamic, thus reload the weight before fully recovering from the fatigue of the body.

This training is aimed at increasing the potential energy sources. Therefore, training is conducted in a way that weight appropriate to the athlete is continually and repeatedly loaded. This training improves mainly the lung function. It enables long bodily action by oxygen intake.

It is desirable to take instable rest or take rest until the heart beat to be downed to 120-140 times per minute.

■ Method

- Set: 8-10 sets
- Frequency: 3 times a week
- Intensity: Heartbeat to be 180 time per minute or higher
- Time of training: 20 minutes

■ Effect

• Improving the endurance of the whole body (heart, lung)
• Improving speed and endurance (speed, agility, muscular endurance)

■ Kinds

• 10m sprint
• Pitching
• Full squat
• Sit up
• Burpee
• Running up and down the stairs
• Footwork (stepping)
• Kicking
• Lying down and standing up

(4) Isometric Training

Isometric training is a kind of muscular training. This is a static training to develop muscles by striking a muscle to the counter muscle or pulling muscles put against a non-moving objects like walls or pillars.

This training can be easily conducted in any place and anytime. This is very effective in Taekwondo which involves many stretching movements.

■ Method

  • Set: 6-10 times
  • Intensity: 6-8 seconds per one time, load the maximum capacity

■ Kinds

  • Level the arm with the shoulder. Give power to fingers and press each other.
  • Level the arm with the shoulder. Give power to fingers and pull each other.
  • Sit before a small box. Pick it up with two feet. This strengthens internal muscles of the foot.
  • Lean one hand against the wall. With the other hand take the ankle of the bent leg of the same side and pull it inside while the foot counteracts.

Chapter 5 FIVE

Tactics

What is tactics?

Tactics is the competitive plan as a method to effectively attack the opponent by forecasting and deciding the competitive situations and executing speedy responses during the process of the competition. In other words, it is a plan for implementation set up to accomplish the goal of the competition by the contestant in each competition.

Tactics is usually grasped during the process of training and is reformed in the process of real competition. To operate tactics a thorough plan has to be previously set up and solutions have to be made according to changing situations during the competition. Prior plan includes a method analyzing the opponent's tactics objectively and a method analyzing it through observation or exercise games. Here, the tactics means the basic purpose of managing the competition. Implementing plan includes technical and psychological methods needed to conduct the competition. The basic unit implementing plan is called an operation.

Tactics in Taekwondo is always relative and thus flexible according to the characteristics of the opponent or the individual. Therefore, general ability should be developed to effectively respond to the changes. Taekwondo competition is a man-to-man competition greatly subject to the effect of the opponent. Prompt decisions (responses) on this ever changing and unexpected competitive situations are needed in

Taekwondo competition.

This ability is divided into prior plan and countermeasures during competition.

① Prior plan

Collecting and analyzing various information on the conditions of the competition and establish a plan. Develop adaptability through practical experience like exercise games.

② Countermeasures during competition

- Prepare alternative plan
- Take the initiative of the game
- Keep one's pace all through the competition
- Moving to the rhythm
- Giving psychological burden to the opponent, etc.

There are repeated situations when the contestant is required to take a special tactical method of action during the competition irrespective of the basic tactical attitude of the opponent and the changing situations of the competition. To solve this kind of task theories and practice of the special tactical basic rules should be grasped. Application ability has to be developed through competition management with various types of opponents.

2

Tactical Actions

■ A method to operate the process of games (contest)
■ To realize one's possibility (specific, mental, technical) as the maximum effect and to overcome the opponent's resistance by spending physical strength efficiently

① Practical factors of tactics:

• Formation and change of technical movements (contest) needed for competition in accordance with the competition rules
• Optimum allocation of power through repeated training corresponding to the real games
• Psychological actions and wilful actions against the opponent

② Process of exhibition of competing ability:

• Confidence: A will for the contest
• Concentration: - Collecting and selecting information
                 - Forecasting and deciding on the situation and prompt execution
• Adaptability: - Appropriate allocation and control of physical strength (throughout 3 rounds)
                - Execution of techniques (timely execution)
                - Execution (coach's directions, selection of

Kyŏrumsae, etc.)
- Ability to manage scoring

③ Extrapolation:

• Prior knowing of the opponent's specialties and habits

④ Understanding the opponent:

• Aggressive type or counteroffensive type?
• Inclined to use right foot or left foot?
• Specialized techniques, feint, etc.?

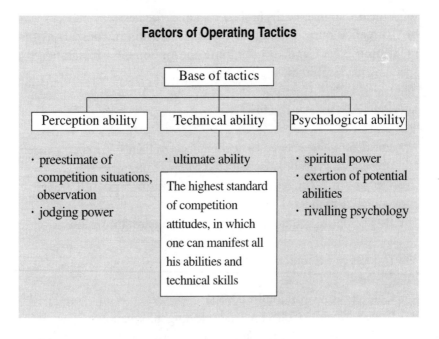

Factors of Operating Tactics

Base of tactics

Perception ability	Technical ability	Psychological ability
· preestimate of competition situations, observation · jodging power	· ultimate ability The highest standard of competition attitudes, in which one can manifest all his abilities and technical skills	· spiritual power · exertion of potential abilities · rivalling psychology

Offensive Actions

Offensive actions are characterized by selecting the target area and initiating active attacks to the opponent in Taekwondo tactics. Offensive actions are mainly executed while moving forward.

All attacks are effective when executed with explosive strength (power) and meet with the tactical needs.

① Types of attacks

Divided into kicks (attacks) and counterkicks (counterattacks) by the order of the execution of offensive techniques.
• Attacks (kicks): Execute single or complex attacks by preemptive attacks to score points
• Counterattacks (counterkicks): Direct execution of techniques or those combined with footwork responding to the opponent's attacks. Single or complex attacks.

② Variations of offensive action

Divided as follows according to the movements of the action and frequency in the process of attacks:
• Feint motion to induce the opponent's attacks
• Single or complex attacks

- Attacks combined with blocks
- Attacks combined with footwork

③ Search for the opponent

Purpose of search is to grasp tactical situation, technical functions, psychological state of physical strength, etc., of the opponent. The followings should be questioned:
- How to respond to a sudden or unexpected attack by the opponent?
- On which factors of attacks we have to put emphasis and how to execute?
- How to take advantage of the time when the opponent is not fully concentrated on the game?
- Conditions of the opponent's physical strength?
- What is the type of the opponent's attacks?
- Is the opponent inclined to keep distance or apt at infighting?
- Techniques preferred by the opponent?

4

Counteroffensive Actions

Counteroffensive actions are used as a method to block the attacking rhythm of the opponent. These are the measurers responding to the opponent's offensive actions and are mainly executed while moving forward. Here, forward action does not simply mean moving ahead. It also includes backward motions in a wider sense.

Counteroffensive actions are not defensive actions. They are a method to accomplish one's attacks taking advantage of the opponent's attacks. They are an advanced level of attacks which require preemptive understanding of all the possibilities of the opponent's unguarded points.

The highest method of counteroffensive action is the counterattack which integrates agility, responsiveness and extrapolation. We can see an excellent contestant keeping the superiority of the contest by breaking the opponent's attacking rhythm and executing counterattacks rather than attacking first.

■ Tips

• Turning or forward stepping is efficient to previously block the attacks by a reckless opponent executing continuous motions.
• Covering from the attacks by frequently used round kick, punch,

etc. is efficient rather than directly blocking the attacking techniques by the opponent.

• The contestant has to establish counterattacking types to be executed in changing situations by understanding the attacking types of the opponent.

• Break the balance of the opponent by feint motion and attack the unguarded points when the opponent mainly executes counterkicks.

5

Tactical Thinking

Tactical thinking plays a decisive role in selecting attacks or counterattack in real competition. Perfection of tactical thinking is an important task in technical, tactical training. Therefore, the level of Taekwondo depends on how hard the contestant consciously think and understand actions during the competition. Effective tactical actions are the expression or the result of complicated process of thinking.

• Tactical thinking means combination of analysis as a method and flexible brain.
• Excellent insight and experienced analysis are required to enable tactical thinking to be creatively active.
• Changes are just the chances.
• Respond resolutely and promptly and take strong initiative in games management while executing changes.

■ Contents of tactical training

• 1st stage: Understanding and analysis of situations of the competition
• 2nd stage: Solution of special tactical tasks by thinking
• 3rd stage: Dynamic solution of tactical tasks, intellectual and physical ability and function

■ Tasks of top priority to obtain tactical effects

• Intensity of basic physical strength and professional physical strength
• Amount of continued training of tactical motions (automation of techniques)
• Ability to catch opportunities
• Ability to execute motions resolutely
• Ability to understand the opponent
• Ability to change the techniques according to the characteristics of the opponent
• Self-possessed management of the competition and confidence
• Ability to execute feint (feint motions, stepping, etc.)

■ Prerequisites to become an excellent athlete

• To be equipped with one's own style of competition by mastering complex special techniques and tactics of his/her own appropriate to his/her ability and condition.
• To manage the competition aggressively. This attitude is a factor to decide win by superiority.
• To take the initiative of the competition by freely respond to any situations of the competition. To effectively manage the competition with any type of opponents, based on 'competition system' characterized by techniques and tactics.

Chapter *6* SIX

Competition

① Competitor and Coach

The relationship between the competitor and the coach is important. The competitor has to trust his/her coach and the coach has to know the competitor's characteristics in detail in every movement of the competitor. The coach plays a decisive role in the competitor's achievement in the competition.

(1) Attitude of the competitor

The competitor must give full play of his/her competitive ability tactically in the competition with the opponent with courage, fair play spirit and strenuosity.

Competitors with different physical conditions and characters show different attitudes to the competition. In general, competitors are divided into three types: offensive type; counteroffensive type; and outfighting type.

• The competitor must realize his/her potential (concrete, spiritual, and technical) and try to win over the opponent with minimum exhaustion.
• The competitor must know that the opponent, when coming near to the boundary line, holds offensive position.
• The competitor must follow the referee's directions faithfully.

- The competitor must draw out the opponent's attacks when the opponent stands close to the boundary line.
- The competitor must lead the competition with active attacks.

(2) Attitude of the coach

① Pre-competition

- The coach must assess and prepare for environmental conditions at the competition site.
- The coach must help the competitor finish warming up and massage fifteen to twenty minutes before the match.
- The coach must analyze the opponent before the match and provide the competitor with tactical advice.
- The coach must help the competitor relax and instill confidence in the outcome of the match.

② During the match

- The coach must analyze the overall competition and the opponent's skill level and give advice to the competitor for the next round during the break inbetween.
- The coach must first cheer the competitor up and give advice during the break between rounds.
- And then, the coach must revitalize the competitor through breathing exercise or active movements.
- The advice given between rounds must be simple and to the point.
- The coach must help the competitor take maximum rest and operate the next round tactically during the break between rounds.
- The coach must refresh the competitor's physical condition by using a sponge on the forehead and the neck and a towel on the face.

③ Post-competition

- The coach must check the physical condition of the competitor for injuries, anxiety or exhaustion.

- The coach must analyze and evaluate the result of the competition.
- The coach must encourage the competitor composedly and warmly regardless of the outcome of the match.
- The coach must help the competitor recover his/her physical condition and restrengthen his/her mind set.
- The coach must advise the competitor to shower with warm water for about 3 minutes and cold water for 1 to 2 minutes and massage the whole body of the competitor strongly to help enhance the blood circulation and recover his/her general physical condition.

2

Weight control

Taekwondo competition is based on weight classes. Therefore, competitors must control their weight. Weight and physical strength are the essential factors in the competitor's successful operation of the match.

■ Tips

• Maintain the optimal weight for best performance, especially through appropriate calorie intake and continued training.
• Use a sauna.
• Obtain medial advice.
• Measure and record weight regularly.

To lose weight, it is desirable to always sweat much during the training and take small water.

Once the competitor reaches the optimal weight, he/she must observe the following cautions to prevent harmful side effects:

• Weight reduction should not exceed more than 5-7 percent of the normal body weight. Otherwise, competitive ability shall be lowered. This has nothing to do with the training condition or the fat of the body.
• To reduce weight, the competitor should not sacrifice good

nutrition. Eat low calorie but nutritious foods (high protein, low fat and carbohydrates).

• Adjust the amount of calories carefully during intensive training periods.

• Excessive limit of water intake may cause malfunction of the body. Drink at least one liter of water daily.

• Take vitamins and minerals through fruits and vegetables. Do not use drugs.

Calorie consumption in training varies in different ages, sexes, and intensity and period of training.

Some competitors use extreme methods to lose weight like taking drugs like diuretics or laxatives, fast, overeating, sweating in a sauna. Excessive intake of diuretics causes the increase in blood sugar which results in headache and lethargy. Excessive weight control weakens internal organs and may cause various side effects like chronic gastritis and anorexia and women's menstrual irregularity.

Sweating, though a bit primitive, is most widely used by athletes of the competition based on weight classes. This enables them to lose weight in a shortest period of time and recover their original weight immediately. However, loss of body fluids exceeding 2-3 percent of the body weight for hours may cause lacking in judgement and optical illusions and exceeding 5 percent of the body weight may cause damage to the membrane and nerves of the brain and disorder in fever metabolism, thus creating a coma.

The seriousness of the problem lies in the fact that weight control is closely related with the outcome of the competition based on weight classes like Taekwondo, judo, boxing and wrestling.

Information

Information about the competition is a method to enhance the efficiency of the competitive ability. It means all data relating to the competition. Collection of various correct and statistical information about the competition is needed.

(1) Systematic collection of information

- Recording on paper or audio recording
- Objective form of observation
- Film or video tape recording

(2) Analysis of information through observation of the competition

- Analysis of the ability and the level of technical standard
- Analysis of the attitude to the competition
- Analysis of the methods to manage the competition (tactics, feint, etc.)

(3) Objectives of collection and analysis of information

① Competitor

- Analysis and correction of weaknesses and mistakes
- Feedback, enhancement and variation of a specific skills

② Opponent

- Prompt information analysis as the situation varies and analysis of the opponent's mistakes and weaknesses
- Improvement of future training in terms of techniques and tactics

Psychological Drill

Psychological drill is a training to strengthen the psychological abilities needed for top performance through enhancing sporting ability to coordinate and change mental and physical techniques. Every sport discipline makes much of this psychological drill as a training to improve sporting ability.

Some athletes do not give full play of their sporting ability in the real competition though they have good physical strength and a good understanding of tactics and show a highly technical skill level and during the training. And some show worse performance in international events than in domestic ones. This shows psychological state of the competitor is as important as the physical, technical and tactical factors.

Regular psychological drill makes the competitor concentrate on the competition only.

Psychological drill needs repeated training like physical training. Therefore, regular training for at least six months is required to obtain its effects.

(1) Mental Training

Mental training is a kind of psychological action in which the process of every movement is done in mind without real action to enable the competitor to learn and improve the movement. This training is very effective in enhancing sporting ability and widely used.

■ Training method

① During the training (in time of learning new techniques)

- Take a calm and comfortable posture.
- Close eyes and take a deep, slow breath while relaxing the body.
- Think clearly the process of the movement of each technique.
- Imagine the process of action.
- Bring up the rapid image of the action.

② Pre-competition

- Take a comfortable posture.
- Close eyes with the mind set.
- Imagine to lead the competition with the opponent.
- Imagine to respond to the opponent's characteristic techniques and tactics.
- Execute analysis between rounds and new tactics.
- Imagine every possible situations of the competition, including attacks and counterattacks, and to successfully manage the competition.
- Imagine to finally win the game.

(2) Meditation

Meditation is to practice Zen to find the truth in Buddhism. Meditation has been done as an essential mental training method in martial arts for a long time. It activates circulation of energy in our body and improves strength, mental force and concentration. Concentration is important to attain victory.

■ Training method

• Take a right posture with legs crossed, the hip backward, and the navel pulled inward.
• Collect force on tanjŏn, the central area of the body approximately two inches below the navel.
• Relax the solar plexus, make the nose and the navel aligned, and take a calm and thin breath while visualizing a word or phrase to focus the attention.

■ Benefits

• Improves mental concentration.
• Helps display one's potential capabilities.
• Develop strong mental force.
• Improves strength, that is power.
• Enhances emotional calmness.

Massage

Massage is very important for competitors at all times. Sport massage should be practiced timely. It is classified as follows;

- Training massage
- Competition massage (pre-competition)
- Between rounds massage
- Post-competition massage (recovery from the fatigue of the competition)

Massage has physical and mental effects. It gives a strong effect to the nervous system. Self-performed massage is a very valuable aid to enhance the competitive ability though its effect lasts shorter than the one performed by a professional. Massage relaxes the muscles and self-performed massage should be the one to make him/her feel refreshed and comfortable. Pressure with the finger tips during massage stimulates the blood vessels and the nerves. Therefore, the pressure should not be strong. Press, shake and rub points of the muscles. Light massage is safer than the strong one.

(1) Stage of massage

- first stage: Pour massage oil or alcohol on the palm of the hand.
- second stage: Rub the specific part of the muscles with the palm

with the pressure intensified gradually.
- third stage: Shake the muscles gently and relax.

Spend five to ten minutes for each specific area, and thirty to forty five minutes for the entire body. Practice massage before the competition. Do not massage during the competition, especially in time of injuries.

(2) Types of massage

- Post-training massage: This is used to promote circulation and to relax the muscles used in training to speed recovery. The best type of post-training massage is deep massage.

- Pre-competition massage: This should be a light and gentle massage to enhance the circulation and prevent cramps. This is a part of warm up and shortens the time for active warm up.

- Between rounds massage: This is a gentle massage to reduce tension of the muscles caused by the strong power loaded during the competition. This is used for speedy recovery and prevention of injuries.

- Post-competition massage: This is used for recovery from the fatigue of the competition and thus to increase the efficiency. This massage should be moderate not to make the contestant feel pain.

Injuries

Sport injuries are the physical injuries incurred during exercise, training or competition. Knowledge of the cause and prevention of injuries enables prevention and rapid recovery from injuries.

Every sport having characteristic techniques can cause various sport injuries. Sport injuries are widely classified as follows: injuries of soft tissue, including skin; injuries of muscles; injuries of tendons; injuries of bones; injuries of joints; and loss of eye sight.

Taekwondo is one of the sports in which competitors are always open to the risk of various injuries during exercise, training and competition. Thus, knowledge of causes and prevention of injuries is essential. The most frequent injuries in Taekwondo are to the toes, instep, knee joints and thigh. Presence of a doctor during the training and competition cannot be too much emphasized.

(1) Major causes of injuries

- Technically unprepared
- Overconfidence
- Overanxiety
- Lack of knowledge
- Inadequate equipment or facilities

• Lack of warm up

(2) Kinds of injuries

• Strain or sprain: A part of muscles or tendons may be torn or cut when they are excessively extended by outer power. Sprain means the sprain of the ligament.
• Tendinitis: Inflammation of the tendon by repeated stimulation.
• Contusion: Damage to the hypodermic tissue by outer power like a think object.
• Laceration: Damage to the skin by outer power like a sharp object.
• Fracture: Loss of continuity of the bone
• Dislocation: The bones of the joint put out of the joint

(3) Causes of injuries

① Classification by forms of injuries:

• Injuries by accidents: fracture, dislocation, strain, and contusion. Injuries in Taekwondo are mainly to the ankle, knee and shoulder.
• Injuries by excessive exercise: tendinitis, inflammation of muscles, arthritis, fracture caused by the fatigue.

② Major causes:

• Internal causes: These relates to age, sex, physical strength and physique of the athlete. Physical causes like muscular power and flexibility.
• Outer causes: Frequency, period, intensity and stability of movement. Causes relating to the sport.
• Environmental causes: Quality of the floor, safety of equipment and whether or not to wear protective equipment.

(4) Prevention

The best way to prevent injuries is to remove all causes of injuries. Primary concern should be given to balanced strengthening of basic physical strength (muscular strength, flexibility and cardiopulmonary endurance).

• Internal prevention: Strengthening of basic physical strength by continued and gradual loading exercise
• Outer prevention: Thorough warming up and winding up before and after competition.
• Environmental prevention: Correct use of equipment and facilities

Measures should be taken immediately in time of injuries and whether or not to continue the contest should be decided.

The following medical supplies are recommended to be prepared for the first aid during daily training or competitions:

• Cool spray
• Adhesive bandages/tapes and gauze
• Ointment or gel
• Massage oil or liniment
• Scissors, tweezers, tripod
• Tourniquet

(5) Symptoms and treatment

① Symptoms:

• Swelling, pain, pressing pain, impediment in movement, bleeding, etc.
• The injured should be sent to a hospital in time of serious injuries like fracture, dislocation or laceration.
• First aid should be given to light injuries like strain, tendinitis or contusion.

② Treatment (RICE therapy)

• Rest: Do not move the injured part of the body in the early stage of sport injuries.
• Ice: Practice ice packing.
• Compression: Wind the injured part with the elastic bandage not so tightly.
• Elevation: Put the injured part higher than the heart.

7

International Competitions

- Olympic Games
  - 2000 Sydney Olympic Games

- International Competitions
  - World Championships
  - World Cup
  - FISU (World University) Taekwondo Championships
  - CISM (World Military) Taekwondo Championships

- Regional Competitions
  - Asian Championships
  - European Championships
  - Pan American Championships
  - African Championships
  - Southeast Asian Championships
  - Arab Championships

- Multi-Sport Games
  - World Games
  - Pan American Games
  - Central American Sports Games
  - Central American & Caribbean Games
  - All Africa Games

- Asian Games
- Southeast Asian Games
- South American Games
- Goodwill Games
- South Pacific Games
- East Asian Games

Appendices

Understanding of Tournament
Amendment of the Competition Rules
Taekwondo Kyŏrugi Terminology
Bibliography

Understanding of Tournament

Various international Taekwondo competitions are being held in different parts of the world today. I often participate as WTF Technical Delegate in those events, where I have found lots of errors made due to incorrect understanding of tournament by the organizing committees themselves. Technical supervision ranges from pointing out any diffusion of the knowledge of tournament to supervision and advice on games management in general. This article is to help readers to understand right what a Taekwondo tournament is and how it works.

■ Origin
The word 'tournament' derived from an equestrian game played between two groups in ancient Greek. It was a man-to-man fight in which an equestrian with a sword and a spear fought against another equestrian and completely armored equestrians on running horses had to have the opponent fall from his horse to be a winner.

■ Meaning
Tournament means elimination tournament. Taekwondo competitions usually adopt tournament system. Competition Rules of the WTF stipulates in Article 6.2 that Taekwondo has two competition systems. One is a single elimination tournament system and the other is round-robin system, that is league system.
Tournament is a system proceeding sports games in which once an

individual or a team loses a match, no further participation in matches is allowed and the winners continue competition mounting one by one the ladder of the pyramid-shaped match tree. The match in which two contestants just under the apex of the pyramid compete for championship is called final, with matches stepwise downward called semifinals and quarter finals and the base of the match tree being the first round. The number of the steps of this match tree is decided by the number of contestants.

League system is different. An individual or a team has matches with every other individual or team participating in the competition. Winners are decided by the percentage of victories to total number of matches.

■ Tournament Management

When contestants number more than four, the number of contestants to compete in the second round shall be four, eight, or sixteen, etc. In the second round, the match in which a bye of the first round is involved should precede the one between winners of the first round.

■ Methods of Making Tournament Table

1. Make the tournament table and then draw lots.

2. Draw lots and make the tournament table based on the principles of making tournament table.

For example, suppose there are six contestants.

[Chart 1]

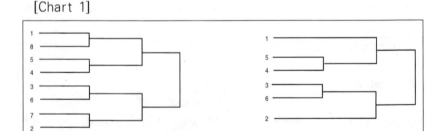

Today, computer programs have been developed so that automatic seeding for tournament is made immediately after simply imputing the numbers drawn.

■ Basic Terms

Knowledge of the following several words is needed for right understanding of tournament.

① Base Number: Number Raised to the Power of 2

These numbers are formal base number in making tournament table. This is the case when the number of participant is 2,4,8,16 or 32, etc. The bracket sheets, the slots on which the names of the contestants are places, must have pair of spaces so as to match up the contestants. The number of positions in a bracket is always a predetermined number. These numbers are 2,4,8,16,32,128, etc. These bracket sizes are by the power of 2. For example, the number 2 raised to the third power $(2 \times 2 \times 2)$ equals 8.

[Chart 2]

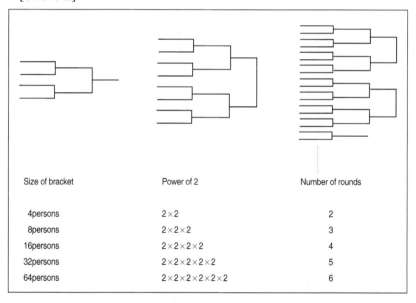

Size of bracket	Power of 2	Number of rounds
4persons	2×2	2
8persons	$2 \times 2 \times 2$	3
16persons	$2 \times 2 \times 2 \times 2$	4
32persons	$2 \times 2 \times 2 \times 2 \times 2$	5
64persons	$2 \times 2 \times 2 \times 2 \times 2 \times 2$	6

* Article 6.3 of the WTC Competition Rules: All international competitions recognized by the WTF shall be formed with participation of at least 3 countries with no less than 3 contestants in each weight class, and any weight class less than 3 contestants cannot be recognized in the official results.

② Match Formation Number: Basic Number Plus One

The sum of the numbers drawn by two contestants in a bracket. Match formation numbers are odd numbers like 3,5,7,9,17,33,129, etc. That is, the number plus one makes the match formation numbers.

[Chart 3]

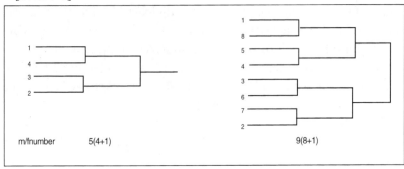

③ Bye Number: Basic Number Minus Number of Participants

Deducting the number of participants out of the basic number closest to and bigger than the number of participants makes the bye number. For example, suppose there are 21 contestants. The basic number closest to 21 among the basic numbers bigger than 21 is 32. 32 minus 21 makes 11. Accordingly, a total of 11 contestants shall become byes in this tournament.

Of course, these byes are decided by drawing. The seeds of these byes shall be located first at the right and left ends of the match tree and be gradually centered as the apex comes nearer.

④ Number of the Opponent: Match Formation Number Minus the Number one Draws

One only has to deduct the number he/she drew out of the matchmaking number to know who is his/her opponent. Imagine total 21 contestants participate in the tournament and you drew the number 17. The basic number becomes 32 and match formation number 33. Thus, you will compete with the contestant numbers 16.

[Chart 4]

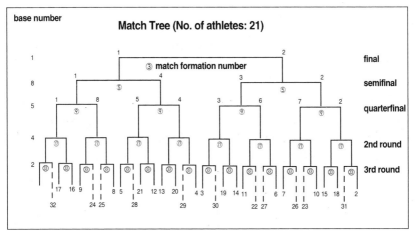

- 1-21: Numbers given to participating contestants
- 22-32: Numbers given to help understand the match formation number

■ Principle

① All participants make pairs from the 1st round of the match tree when the number of participants (individuals or teats) is by the power of 2 which are base numbers like 2,4,8,16 or 32, etc.

② The first round of the match tree includes bye(s) if the number of participants is not 2 or the power of 2. By doing so, the number of contestants int he second round can be 2 or the power of 2 and two contestants or two teams can compete in the final.

③ The numbering of each slot in tournament table is made according to the match formation number such as 3,5,9,17,33, etc. That is, the number of the total slots in the first round is the closest match formation number bigger than the number of participants.

④ The pertinent base number minus the number of byes makes the number of pairs in the first round. Here, the sum of the number drawn of one contestant plus the number drawn of his/her opponent is the match formation number.

The statements above are the knowledge needed for overall understanding of tournament. Analysis of the tournament table with knowledge of basic terms and principles would lead to easy understanding of tournament matchmaking. One holding a black belt Tan grade should have full knowledge of tournament, which will improve the atmosphere of Taekwondo competitions. (WTF Taekwondo No.58/1996)

Amendment of the Competition Rules

In accordance with Article 19 of the Rules and Regulations, the amendment of the Competition Rules is proposed as follows;

Article	Existing Rules	Proposed Amendment
Article 3 Competition Area	2-3) Position of the Head of Court The position of the Head of Court shall be marked at least 100cm away from the Boundary Line facing the referee's Mark.	To be deleted
Article 4.2 The costume for Contestants	2) The contestant shall wear the trunk protector, groin guard, forearm and shin guards before entering the contest area, and the groin guard, forearm and shin guards shall be worn inside the Taekwondo uniform. The female contestant shall wear the trunk protector, head	2) The contestant shall wear the trunk protector, head protector, groin guard, forearm and shin guards before entering the contest area and the groin guard, forearm and shin guards shall be worn inside the Taekwondo uniform, and the contestant shall bring the

Article	Existing Rules	Proposed Amendment
	protector, women's groin guard, women's breast guard, forearm and shin guards before entering the contest area, and women's groin guard, women's breast guard, forearm and shin guards shall be worn inside the Taekwondo uniform.	protectors for personal use.
	3) The contestant shall wear the contestant's number or the back of the uniform.	To be deleted
Article 4.3 Medical Control	2)The WTF may carry out any medical testing deemed necessary to ascertain if a contestant has committed a breach of this rule, and any winner who refuses to undergo this testing or who proves to have committed such a breach shall be removed from the final standings.	2) The WTF may carry out medical testing deemed necessary to ascertain if contestant has committed a breach of this rule, and any winner who refuses to undergo this testing or who proves to have committed such a breach shall be removed from the final standings, and the record shall be transferred to the contestant next in line in the competition standings **The following to be added** 3) The organizing committee shall be liable for arrangements to carry out medical testion

Article	Existing Rules	Proposed Amendment
Article 5 Weight Division	2.Weight divisions are divided as follows	2. Weight divisions are divided as follows

w/category	Male division		w/category	Male division
Fin	Not exceeding 50kg		Fin	Not exceeding 54kg
Fly	Over 50kg & not exceeding 54kg		Fly	Over 54kg & not exceeding 58kg
Bantam	Over 54kg & not exceeding 58kg		Bantam	Over 58kg & not exceeding 62kg
Feather	Over 58kg & not exceeding 64kg		Feather	Over 62kg & not exceeding 67kg
Light	Over 64kg & not exceeding 70kg		Light	Over 67kg & not exceeding 72kg
Welter	Over 70kg & not exceeding 76kg		Welter	Over 72kg & not exceeding 78kg
Middle	Over 76kg & not exceeding 83kg		Middle	Over 78kg & not exceeding 84kg
Heavy	Over 83kg		Heavy	Over 84kg

w/category	Female division		w/category	Female division
Fin	Not exceeding 43kg		Fin	Not exceeding 47kg
Fly	Over 43kg & not exceeding 47kg		Fly	Over 47kg & not exceeding 51kg
Bantam	Over 47kg & not exceeding 51kg		Bantam	Over 51kg & not exceeding 55kg
Feather	Over 51kg & not exceeding 55kg		Feather	Over 55kg & not exceeding 59kg
Light	Over 55kg & not exceeding 60kg		Light	Over 59kg & not exceeding 63kg
Welter	Over 60kg & not exceeding 65kg		Welter	Over 63kg & not exceeding 67kg
Middle	Over 65kg & not exceeding 70kg		Middle	Over 67kg & not exceeding 72kg
Heavy	Over 70kg		Heavy	Over 72kg

Article	Existing Rules	Proposed Amendment
		The following to be added 3. Weight divisions for the olympic games are divided as follows **Male division** Not exceeding 58kg Over 58kg & not exceeding 68kg Over 68kg & not exceeding 88kg Over 80kg **Female division** Not exceeding 49kg Over 49kg & not exceeding 57kg Over 57kg & not exceeding 67kg Over 67kg
Article 6 Classification and Method of Competition	2) Team competition Systems of competition • Five (5) contestants with no weight limit	2) Team Competition: Systems of Competition 1) Five (5) contestants by weight classification with the following category **Male division** Not exceeding 54kg Over 54kg & not exceeding 68kg Over 63kg & not exceeding 80kg Over 72kg & not exceeding 82kg Over 82kg

Article	Existing Rules	Proposed Amendment
		Female division
		Not exceeding 49kg Over 47kg & not exceeding 54kg Over 54kg & not exceeding 61kg Over 63kg & not exceeding 68kg Over 68kg
		To be added
		3) Taekwondo competition of the olympic game shall be conducted individual competition system between contestants
	3. All international-level competitions recognized by the WTF shall be formed with participation of at least 3 countries with no less than 3 contestants in each weight class, and any weight class with less than 3 contestants cannot be recognized in the official results	3. All international-level competition recognized by the WTF shall be formed with participation of at least 4 countries with no less than 4 contestants cannot be recognized in the official results
Article 9 Weigh in	2. Weigh-in shall be conducted in teh nude.	2. During weigh-in, the male contestant shall wear underpants and the females contestant shall wear underpants and brassiers. However, weigh-in may be conducted in the nude un the case that the contestant

Article	Existing Rules	Proposed Amendment
		wishes to co so.
Article 10 Procedures of the contest	2. Physical and costume inspection After being called, the contestants shall undergo physical and costume inspection at the designated inspection desk, and the contestant shall not show any signs of aversion, and also shall not bear any materials which could cause harm to the other contestant.	2. Physical and costume inspection After being called, the contestants shall undergo physical and costume inspection at the designated inspection desk by the inspection cesignated by the wtf, and the contestant shall not show any signs of aversion, and also shall not bear any materials which could cause harm to the other contestant.
Article 14 Prohibited Acts	6. Prohibited acts: Kyŏng-go penalty 1) Grabbing the opponent 2) Pushing the opponent with the shoulder, body, hands or arms 3) Holding the opponent with the hands or arms 4) Internationally crossing the Alert Line 5) Evading by turning the back to the opponent 6) Internationally falling down 7) Pretending injury 8) Attacking with the knee 9) Attacking the groin intentionally	6. Prohibited acts: kyŏng-go penalty 1) Touching acts A. Grabbing the oppoent B. Holding the oppoent C. Pushing the oppoent D. Touching the opponent with the trunk 2) Negative acts A. Intentionally crossing the alere line B. Evaning turning the back to the opponent C. Intentionally falling doun D. Pretending injury 3) Attacking acts

Article	Existing Rules	Proposed Amendment
	10) Intentionally stomping or kinking any part of the leg or foot 11) Hitting the opponent's face with hands or fist 12) Gesturing to indicate scoring or deduction by raising hands, etc. 13) Uttering undesirable remarks or any misconduct on the part of the contestant or the coach	A. Butting or attacking with the knee B. Intentionally attacking the groin C. Intentionally stamping face with hands part of the leg or foot D. Hitting the opponent's face with hands or fists 4) Undesirable acts A. Gesturing to indicate scoring or deduction on the part of the contestant or the coach B. Uttering undesirable remarks or any misconcuct on the part of the contestant or the coach C. Leaving the cosignated mark on the part of the coach during match
	7. Prohibited acts: Kamchŏm Penalty 1) Attacking the fallen opponent 2) Intentionally attacking after the Referee's declaration of "kalyŏ" (break) 3) Attacking the back and the back the back of the head intentionally 4) Attacking the opponent's face severely with hands or fist	7. Prohibited acts: Kamchŏm Penalty 1) Touching acts A. Throwung the opponent B. Intentionally throwung cown the opponent by grappling the opponent's attacking foot in the air with the arm 2) Negative acts A. Crossing the boundary line B. Intentionally interffring

Article	Existing Rules	Proposed Amendment

	5) Butting
	6) Crossing the Boundary Line
	7) Throwing the opponent
	8) Violent or extreme remarks or behavior on the part of the contestant or the coach
		with the progress of the match
		3) Attacking acts
		  A. Attacking the fallen opponent
		  B. Intentionally Attacking the back and the back of the head
		  C. Attacking the opponent's face severely with hands
		4) Undesirable acts
		Violent or extreme remarks or behavior on the part of the contestant or the coach

Article 21 Head of court	1. Qualification Holder or International Referee certificate with years of experience in competition management	To be deleted
	2. Duties 1) Overall control and supervision of the pertinent competition area 2) Confirmation of the decision 3) Evaluation of the Referee's and judge's performance 4) Giving a report at any meeting of the Board of Arbitration	To be deleted

Article	Existing Rules	Proposed Amendment
Article 23 Assignment of officials	1.Composition of officials 1) in the use of non-electronic trunk protector: The officials are composed of one Head of Court, one Referee and four Judges 2) In the use of electronic trunk protectors: The officials are composed of one Head of Court, one Referee and two Judges. 2. Assignment of Officials 1) The assignment of the Head of Court, The Referees and Judges shall be made after the contest schedule is fixed. 2) Referees and Judges with the same nationality as that of either contestant shall not be assigned to such a contest. However, an exception shall be made for the Judges when the absolute number of the Referees and Judges is wholly insufficient.	1. Composition of reffreeing officials 1) In the use of non-electronic trunk protector: The officials are composed of one Referee and three Judges. 2) In the use of electronic trunk protectors: The officials are composed of one Referee and two Judges 2. Assignment of reffreeing officials 1) The assignment of the Referee and Judges shall be made after the contest schedule is fixed. 2) Referees and Judges with the same nationality as that of either contestant shall not be assigned to such a contest. However, an exception shall be made for the Judges when the number of refereeing officials is insufficient as the case may be

Article	Existing Rules	Proposed Amendment
Article 24 Other matters not specified in the Rules	In the case that any matters not specified in the Rules occur, they shall be dealt with as follows; 1) Matters related to the competition shall be decided through consensus by the Head of Court and the refereeing officials of the pertinent contest. 2) Matters which are not related to a specific contest, shall be decided by the Executive Council or its proxy	In the case that any matters not specified in the Rules occur, they shall be dealt with as follows; 1) Matters related to the competition shall be decided through consensus by the refereeing officials of the pertinent contest. 2) Same as the existing Rules To be added 3) The organizing committee shall prepare for a video tape recorder at each court for recording and preservation of the match process
Article 25 Arbitration	4. Other provisions A video tape recorder shall be set up at each court for deliberation of the protest Proposed Amendment	To be deleted

Taekwondo kyŏrugi terminology

A

apch'uk	ball of foot

C

ch'agi	kick
ch'aechŏmp'yo	judging paper
ch'aryŏt	attention
chayu kyŏrugi	free sparring
ch'egŭp	weight division
chitki	footwork, step
ch'ŏng	blue
ch'ŏng sŭng	blue wins
chunbi	ready
chushim	referee
chwa-u-hyang-u	face each other, face to face

H

hoejŏn	round
- il hoejŏn	- first round
- i hoejŏn	- second round
- sam hoejŏn	- third round
hogu	chest protector, trunk protector
hong	red

hong sŭng	red wins
hoshinsul	self-defense
huryŏ ch'agi	whip kick, crescent kick

ⓚ

kallyŏ	break
kamdokkwan	head of court
kamchŏm	deduction point
kibon	basic
kihap	yelling
kikkwŏn	withdrawal
kisul	technique
- chŏnmun kisul	- professional technique
- kibon kisul	- basic technique
kŏdŭp ch'agi = iŏ ch'agi	continuous kicking
kongkyŏk	attack
- chejari kongkyŏk	- in-place attack
- chikchŏp kongkyŏk	- direct attack
- kanjŏp kongkyŏk	- indirect attack
- kiŏoru kongkyŏk	- incline attack
- mikkŭro kongkyŏk	- sliding attack
- tanil kongkyŏk	- single attack
kullŏ chitki	drawing footwork
kyeshi	count time
kyesok	continue
kyŏnggi	competition
kyŏnggijang	competition site
kyŏnggo	warning
kyŏnggye son	boundary line
kyŏngrye	bow
kyŏrugi	sparring/fighting
kyŏrumsae	fighting stance
- ap kyŏrumsae	- front fighting stance
- orŭn kyŏrumsae	- right-handed stance
- oen kyŏrumsae	- left-handed stance
- yŏp kyŏrumsae	- side fighting stance

M

mach'wo kyŏrugi	arranged sparring
makki	block
- arae makki	- low section block
- momt'ong makki	- middle section block
- ŏlgul makki	- high section block
mullŏ chitki	backward footwork

N

naeryŏ ch'agi	downword kick
naga chitki	forward footwork
natch'umsae	low fighting stance

P

p'anjŏng	decision
p'ihagi	avoiding

S

satpodae	groin guard
shigan	time
shihap	competition
shijak	begin/start
shilkyŏk	disqualification
shimp'an judge	

T

tch'ikŏ ch'agi = naeryŏ ch'agi	downward kick
tch'irŭgi	punch

U

usae	superiority

Y

ye	courtesy
yonggu	equipment
yŏllimsae	open stance

④

Bibliography

• Berndt Barth and another, Fechten. Berlin: Sportverlag, 1979
• Chae Hong-won and 2 others (co-ed.), Theory of Elites Sports Training. Seoul: Bokyong Munhwasa, 1992
• Choi Yong-ryol, Theory of Taekwondo Kyorugi. Seoul: Samhak Publishing Co., 1989
• Gerhard Lehmann and another, Judo. Berlin: Sportvelag, 1983
• Harre, Trainingslehre. Berlin: Sportverlag, 1986
• Horst Fiedler and another, Boxsport. Berlin: Sportverlag, 1980
• Jurgen Hartmann and 2 others, Ringen. Berlin: Sportverlag, 1980
• Kim Dae-keon, Theories and Actualities of Sports Studies. Seoul: Seonil Munhwasa, 1988
• Kim Jin-won, Theory of Training. Seoul: Tonghwa Munhwasa, 1988
• Kim Jong-hun and 2 others (co-ed.), Methodology of Training. Seoul: Teaching Research Press, 1990
• Kang Man-su (tr.), Toward MVP. B&R, 1992
• KTA, Taekwondo Quarterly No.85. Seoul: Korea Taekwondo Association, 1993
• Kukkiwon, Taekwondo Textbook, 1989
• Ku Je-yon, Theory of Coaching. Seoul: Hyongseol Publishing Co., 1991
• Kyong Myong Lee, Richtig Taekwondo. Munich: BLV, 1987
• _____, Taekwondo. Warsaw: Alma Press, 1989

- _____ and another, Taekwondo Kyorugi. Seoul: Oh-seong Publishing, 1996
- Matwejew, Grundlagen des Sportlichen Training. Berlin: Sportverlag, 1980
- M. Grosser and 2 others, Kongditionstraining. Munich: Sportwissen, 1981
- _____ and 2 others, Leistungssteuerung. Munich: Sportwissen, 1986
- _____ and another, Techniktraing. Munich: Sportwissen, 1986
- Park Hui-seon, Daily-life Zen Meditation. Seoul: Spiritual World Press, 1992
- Sportmassage. Wien: Bflw, 1986
- WTF, International Referee Seminar-Study Materials, 1992
- Encyclopedia of Physical Education. Seoul: Jinbo Publishing, 1995
- Young-oak Kim, Principles Governing the Construction of the Philosophy of Taekwondo. Seoul: Tongnamu Publishing, 1995

Dynamic Taekwondo

— a Martial Art & Olympic Sport

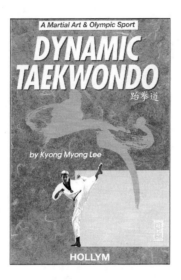

Taekwondo is one of the most popular sports
among many foreigners in the world
as well as Korean people.
It is a sport contributing to the health and fitness
both in body and spirit.

Author sums up the unique dynamism of his sports:
"The ultimate winner is the one who conquer himself."
Dynamic Taekwondo presents all you need to know
about Taekwondo from its history to the basic stance and
many of the movesand skills employed.

Hardcover / ISBN: 1-56591-060-5